The Collapse of the

Three Story Universe

Christianity in an Age of Science

Daniel Wolpert

a MICAH Book

D1490510

Cover Drawing by Trey Everett

Minnesota Institute of Contemplation and Healing
Crookston MN 56716
www.micahprays.org

I have been blessed with many great teachers in my life. This book is dedicated to them all. In the fields of science and contemplation I particularly lift up:

Travis Solomon
Len Kelly
Tarthang Tulku
Pema Chodren
Bede Griffiths

You all helped me glimpse reality as it is.

Table of contents

Introduction

The most important things in life are invisible. They occur without our giving them a thought. Our brain runs, our heart pumps blood, and our intestines digest food, all via processes unknown to our conscious mind. Similarly, our thoughts, feelings, our very Self, are invisible yet essential to our existence. Our most basic assumptions about reality, life, and culture, are also unseen. Yet we could not function without them. We assume that people around us will speak a certain language when we talk to them, we assume that electricity will come out of three holes in the wall, we assume that certain functions will occur in the buildings we visit every day, and that those we talk to will understand basic cultural references.

We get a glimpse of this invisible world, whenever one of these assumptions breaks down, if even for an instant. For example, perhaps you've had the experience of being in a moving vehicle when for one second, really a fraction of a second, you look out a window and it appears to you that the world, not you, is moving. Of course this illusion disappears instantaneously, but that instant when the world seems quite different is enough to create an uneasy feeling in your stomach.

Another such example is when our gaze rests on a piece of wood, or stone and suddenly we glimpse a face. In that moment we mistake an inanimate object for one that is alive. Again the illusion passes quickly, but when we so misjudge an object, we are disoriented and even afraid.

These are fleeting examples, but there also are more permanent situations that defy our 'normal' understanding of how things are. Holy sites exist where people claim to be healed in miraculous ways or see visions of God. Then there are certain objects or phenomenon whose existence is somehow labeled 'mysterious' because they fall outside our current understanding. One such example are the huge statues on Easter Island. Although recently some scientists claim they understand how these faces were made, when I was a child, they were still labeled as a mystery. Some people even insisted that aliens had put them there because it wasn't clear how islanders with no mechanical technology could have built the statues.

The practice of science is a method for analyzing material, even cultural, phenomenon that aren't yet understood. Apart from the scientific method, the reactions, by the average person, to new or mysterious objects, occurrences, or changes in cultural assumptions tend to fall in one of two general categories. The first response is something like: "I don't want to think about that." A person with this attitude retreats from the object as if it were dangerous or even seeks to eliminate it from the world.

One modern example of this reaction is how many Americans respond to new immigrants speaking languages other than English. Many white Americans have the cultural assumption that in America, everyone should speak only one language. Of course this is just a cultural assumption and bias, not some great objective truth. In most countries and cultures many languages are spoken and understood without anyone getting upset. However when this invisible cultural assumption is challenged in America, many become very angry and hostile because they are encountering what for them is a mysterious new practice.

The second category of reaction is to assume that some explanation will be found that fits the person's current understanding of how things are. Once they have found an idea that suits them, they declare the problem solved and relax, even if their explanation doesn't actually fit the new reality before their eyes. One can hear this attitude expressed when someone who isn't religious is confronted with some data about a 'spiritual' occurrence. In this situation such a person often says something like, "Well science will explain that someday." This pronouncement can be followed by a lack of interest in any further conversation.

Rarely, very rarely, there is a third reaction that accepts the fact of the strange situation and seeks a brand new explanation that more closely correlates with the new data.

This need for invisible assumptions reveals humans to be somewhat analogous to computers. A computer has software that runs in the background of every program. Right now, I am typing this sentence on a computer in a word processing program. As I type, millions of bits of information zoom through the circuits of my laptop beyond my awareness. These bits of information make my typing on the screen possible, and without them I couldn't be performing this task, yet they are invisible to me. In the same way, people are programmed from birth, really from before birth, with physical, psychological, social, and cultural information that allows them to function and is also largely invisible to them. When this information is threatened with change, our system, just like our computer, 'crashes'. We feel confused and uncertain. We are scared and disoriented, and we try, in several clearly defined ways, to 'reboot' our system, to restore balance and once again function as before.

Religion is grounded in many basic, often invisible, assumptions about the universe. Most people in the Western world were raised with certain images of God and material reality[1], the universe in which we find ourselves, that come from what we call the Judeo-Christian tradition.   For centuries, these assumptions were so embedded in most people's consciousness that they were invisible to the average person.

However, over the past 500 or so years another set of images about material reality has been generated, and these contradict many of the fundamental images of the religions of the West.   Having two contrasting and contradicting images within the same cultural arena has created a crisis in many circles of our society.   But because our assumptions are often invisible to us, we may be unclear what exactly we are in crisis about, or if we are clear, then it is hard to discuss this crisis openly with others because the invisible software keeps crashing and creating problems.

The two competing sets of images I am referring to are what I will call the 'Three-Story Universe' model of material reality and the 'Scientific' model of material reality.

The first, is the view of the world that comes to us[2] through what is called 'Scripture'.   Depending on what

---

[1] In this book when I use the term 'reality' I am referring to our material reality, that is the place and condition where we seem to find ourselves when we wake up each morning. I realize that 'reality' can also refer to such things as socially constructed norms and values, psychological states, metaphors for life, constructed narratives, opinions etc. This is not what I am referencing when I use this word. Sometimes I will use the phrase 'material reality' or 'the universe' to remind the reader what I mean by this term.

[2] in this book the 'us' I am referring to are those peoples who have been influenced or formed by what is sometimes referred to as the Judeo-Christian tradition. Muslims have been formed by the same scripture and world view and so could possibly be included in this 'us'.

religion you subscribe to this Scripture is either called the Torah or the Old Testament. In this Scripture, the universe is like a three-story building. There is the Earth in the middle, with an upstairs, the Heavenly Realms, and a downstairs, either Hell or the Realm of the Dead. In this view the upstairs is where God lives and after their death people go either up or down, or both, depending on the specifics of one's faith. God is a person living upstairs, along with lots of other heavenly beings, and these non-human beings have access to earth in a way that we don't have access to heaven.

The second view is the one that is taught in every school in the western (and most of the eastern) world. In this view, the earth is a round planet that orbits the sun, a small star, in the corner of a galaxy - a place full of stars. The universe is huge and mostly empty. So far, we haven't found any other life forms in this big universe, nor have they found us, that we know of, but it is increasingly assumed that there are other planets like ours that could contain life in some form.

Obviously these two images, taken literally, have little in common. Our response to this lack of commonality has gone in several predictable directions - much like the reactions to the mysterious objects and occurrences. The most common is that people pick one or another image and use that whenever it is most convenient. So when in church, people are fine with the Three-Story universe image, but when they are watching the moon-landing, they prefer the scientific image. Another approach is to pick one and reject the other. This is more common for people who have left organized religion on the one hand, or people who belong to what have been loosely labeled fundamentalist faiths on the other. The former are happy with what they see as the truth of the scientific view, the latter advocate for the truth of the Three-Story Universe view.

These approaches all have their challenges and problems. The first (switching images as needed) results in a problematic feeling of inconsistency and confusion. How can one image of reality be 'correct' on Sunday morning and 'wrong' on Tuesday night? The second (picking one or another) is problematic in that neither image, as classically portrayed in popular culture and use, is complete or consistent. On the one hand, no one 'really' believes the three-story image no matter how much they act like they do, on the other hand, a cold deterministic view of the universe not only feels very empty and meaningless but it also appears to be contradicted by the same science that created it (more on this in the chapters that follow). But there is a third option.

Returning to the computer analogy, we know that when our software gets sufficiently old and obsolete there are many things that we simply cannot do with our computer. For example, older copies of internet browser software won't allow us to view video on the internet. Crippled by the old code we can lurch along with our outdated programs, as we often do for awhile, or we can get rid of that software and get new versions. When we buy a new program, it doesn't mean that we have stopped using computers, it means that we are getting a new tool so that we can continue to use the machine in a new way.

Recently there has been an explosion of books, articles, and information on the nature of the universe and our place in it. These books have tried to provide a new image or images, about the nature of reality that fit more closely with what we know about the universe and about ourselves. These books are not simply a rehash of either the Three-Story Universe or the pre-21st century scientific world view, but rather they are something different. They try to present a new view, and often they discuss how at odds this new view is from the 'traditional' - i.e. highly deterministic, materialistic, non-spiritual - 'scientific' community.

These books come from both outside and inside the Christian faith community, and are written by a wide array of people including physicists, other scientists, journalists, all of whom may also be a member of any number of faith communities.

Within the Christian Church, the reaction to this discussion is mixed due to the three different reactions to new views of reality I described above. Many Christians don't wish to participate in this conversation because it is too unnerving. Like the strange disorientation that occurs when you think the world is moving while your car stands still, people raised within the Three-Story Universe world feel scared and disoriented when they talk about a new view of reality. On the other hand, those who don't feel distressed often are silent because they either don't wish to get into an argument with someone, or they don't feel that they have a clear model to describe how the Christian world view and the scientific world view come together. This mix of responses, as well as the extreme hostility of some to any attempt to rework the Three-Story Universe concept, has meant that, in the vast majority of church settings, the Three-Story Universe has endured - even if unspoken - because it's the default model, simple and easy to articulate.

This book is a contribution to the discussion of a new vision of reality. From a Christian perspective I will describe a model of reality that the average person can understand and is true to the state of our current scientific knowledge. The form of this work is primarily theological. Rather than beginning with a description of quantum mechanics for the lay person (as many of these other works do) and then moving to some vision of how mind and matter interact, I want to begin from the perspective of the Christian faith, incorporate a non Three-Story Universe reality, and see where we come out on the other side.

Such a discussion will be useful on several fronts. One is for the person of faith inside the church who may, consciously or unconsciously, be anxious about discussing a faith built upon a model of reality, the Three-Story Universe, they know to be false. I believe that if this person had another more consistent model or image to draw from they would be more confident about being a person of faith in the modern world.

Hopefully this work will also be of help to the thousands of people who have left the church precisely because they can no longer deal with a faith based upon an image of material reality that is untrue. Perhaps if they had an image of faith and reality that was more consistent they would be able to reconnect with their faith lives in a more meaningful way.

Finally, I hope that this work will be useful in interfaith dialogue. People of different faiths continue to kill one another by the thousands often because of differences in doctrine and dogma. But what if the images of our faith began to derive from the common image of the universe that we all, whether we are willing to admit it or not, share? Perhaps we could begin to relate to each other from a stance and posture that was more peaceful.

As I close this introduction I want to make explicit two working assumptions that are essential to this work; both of these assumptions have to do with the methods I use to come to this new model of material reality.

The first highlights the importance of contemplation, or the practice of the direct examination of our mind, as we seek to understand the world. We often forget that our mind exists because it is so central to everything we do. However for thousands of years the contemplative disciplines have offered a powerful, consistent method for examining reality. If we are going to try and understand how God fits into a material reality that is described by science, then I think the practice of contemplation, which is also a method of observing reality, will be very helpful. Thus, although I will not necessarily discuss contemplation directly, many of my observations about humanity, the material world, and God come out of this tradition; and I will be referring to this perspective in some of the examples given in the book.

The second assumption is that I am not afraid of thinking or of the exploration and advancement of knowledge. Although scientists think of themselves as embracing this assumption, I find that there are people both inside and outside the church who wish to limit thinking and curiosity. Inside the church I certainly find it necessary to be clear about such a stance relative to knowledge. This is true because many people who wish to be committed Christians and people of faith, approach the issue of the nature of reality in the same way that some react to mysterious objects: "I don't want to think about it." or, even more radically, "thinking about it is bad." This is an approach I cannot condone whether it comes from people of faith or from those who call themselves scientists. If Jesus is indeed 'the truth' then knowledge and truth are good things and, if followed rigorously, they can only lead us, eventually, to a state of being that is commensurate with what Jesus stands for and who He is.

As you read the chapters that follow, allow your mind to drift freely though the ideas and images on the page. Remember that this description of reality isn't reality itself. Rather it is one possible vision that hopefully brings together some of what we know today with some of what the Christian faith has taught for many years. And as you read you may ask yourself if this new presentation rings true to your experience and to the stirrings of your heart, and helps you to imagine an in-Spirited universe alive with the presence of the Divine.

Chapter 1

The Earth

"Where is God if we can't see Him?" This question has been asked, and rarely answered, at inconvenient moments of many a children's sermon. In the 21st century, with our telescopes, space stations, particle accelerators, knowledge of biology, medicine and natural disasters, it is also a question that persistently knocks at the door of the minds of millions. The ancient image of material reality, enshrined and encoded on the ceiling of the Sistine Chapel no longer holds sway in our society. Yet it's still the dominant model of reality presented in most Sunday schools and embedded in the language and images of most church services.

On billboards, tee-shirts, bumper stickers, and even commercials, the conflicts that rage over topics related to this simple question gather hours of media attention, and thousands of pages of paper and electronic print. As a world, we are concerned with where and how God does, or doesn't, fit into the universe described by modern science.

The purpose of this book is to try to present a series of images that will allow us to understand how it is indeed possible for an invisible being to be part of our material reality in a manner that is both significant and consistent with what we currently understand about that reality.[3] As I discussed in the introduction, this work is organized along theological lines, using theological categories from the Christian faith as a framework on which to paint this new image. This exploration also relies on contemplative practice and teachings as a method for examining reality, as the spiritual tradition will help us see all things new.

Contemplation starts with our experience of the world. We begin our spiritual practice by attending to our thoughts and feelings. Who are we? What is the world? Following this tradition, I will also begin with our experience and the doctrine of Creation. From there I move to other theological categories, always linking experience, science, and the descriptions of faith offered by Christianity. Thus let's begin with what people, both ancient and modern, find when they start their day.

Every morning we wake up and find ourselves in an amazing place we call the earth. We experience this earth as flat. The horizon stretches out in every direction like a giant disk (unless there are mountains in the way) and no matter how far we go, the horizon is always there and we remain upright upon the ground. Above us, is a blue space that

---

[3] Throughout this work I make reference to the conflicts between science and faith. While I am very aware that there are also people who don't see a conflict between these two realms of human activity, in our culture the conflict, as I mentioned, gets the most press and is the most vocal. Because of this visibility, the conflict can take center stage in people's minds. Furthermore, people who don't sense a conflict often don't have a way of articulating the lack of conflict. To construct a 'conflict-free' model is the purpose of this work. See the Introduction for a more detailed discussion of the various responses to the interaction between science and faith.

appears curved like a dome. It's not so hard to imagine something above that dome, as well as something below the flat ground. Given this state of affairs, we can't fault our Biblical ancestors for envisioning the world as they did.

The Heavenly Realms were up and above the dome of the sky, the Earth was a flat disk on which we stood, and below this disk was the Realm of the Dead. This model of the universe is called the Three-Story Universe (TSU), and this basic ancient view has endured within the Church and in the minds of believers, both consciously and unconsciously, for centuries. It endures, at least in part, because it's a description of reality that is consistent with our everyday experience.

As we continue to explore this incredible 'earth' that is our home, we find that there are many different objects here. Some appear stable and mostly unchanging, but some change dramatically; they move and grow and make more of themselves, just like us. The world is divided into living and non-living things and each type appears separate and distinct. Larger, visible, living things mate with their own kinds and reproduce new creatures similar in form to their parents. Again, as we examine our experience it fits very well with the basic Biblical description of the world.

Then we realize that we are here! This is an obvious statement but it's very important. Slowly we recognize our unique ability to be aware of our presence. We 'know' that there is a world here in a way that no other living thing knows. We have the ability to describe reality, to be curious about it, to categorize and name and calculate and record. We have a mind that is aware and this property and skill sets us apart from everything else in the earth and gives us the power to manipulate and change the world in ways that no other creature can. We can make choices and use our awareness.   By virtue of this particular attribute, the earth appears to be 'ours.'   Again our experience mimics the Biblical assertion that we have 'dominion' over the world.

At the same time, we realize we didn't make this place in which we find ourselves. We just woke up and here we are! We didn't make the creatures, or even the non-life forms, and furthermore we have no idea how this all got here. We also have some dim notion that things were here before we were. Just as our parents and grandparents tell us of times that came before we were alive, we can imagine, and perhaps even have some sense of, a time before anyone's parents were here. So not only do we experience the spatial quality of our earth, but we also experience and are aware of its temporal nature. We know of the existence of time, knowledge that's also made possible by our minds.

Our experience of both time and space gives rise to the experience of Creation; of the coming into being of the place we inhabit. We exist within a Created order. Somehow, in some way, all of what lies before us has been created, or has come into being. And it wasn't created by us.

Simply by looking at our experience we have arrived at one of the core Doctrines of our faith: Creation. We exist within a world that is not of our own making. The earth is a gift if you will; because on the one hand it's ours, but on the other hand we didn't make it, and if it vanished we couldn't reproduce it. But there is one more step.

As we continue to look around and have a sense of the earth going back into time, it's quite natural to ask, "How did this all get here?" "How did Creation happen?" In ancient times, as people pondered this question, the most logical answer was that someone, with a mind much like ours only better, created everything. Because as we look around, we can see that the individual things of this world, while remarkable, can only make more of themselves. A fly can't make a cow. The only creature that can make lots of different new things is us! We can make houses and pots and chariots and temples and clothes and other items that never existed before.

Therefore we can understand the impulse, common to every human society in some form, to say that whatever created this world must have a mind similar to ours, but also vastly superior, for the earthly creation is incredible beyond anything we could make. The creature with this mind is God. And this is the full doctrine of Creation; a model of our world that, contrary to what some theologians have claimed, is quite in sync with both our basic experience and the Biblical witness.

However, knowledge of the created world didn't end with our basic experience. Time passed and humanity began to learn more about the earth; we continue to be very curious. And even though our day to day experience of the world doesn't change all that much, our knowledge about this experience changes tremendously. On the face of it, what we've learned over the centuries could reinforce and support the doctrine of Creation. We have learned that everything in the universe is interconnected at every level of reality. Rather than being a place of separate or perhaps different creations, the universe is 'One', as if it was made by the same being. Furthermore, life is beautiful and miraculous. All creatures that inhabit the planet are exquisitely put together; remarkable beyond anything we could imagine; and they are living, the most amazing thing of all. Our developing knowledge should have been a good thing for our faith for indeed the Creation appears to be 'very good.'

Yet change and newness cause trouble. As our knowledge of the universe grew, the Christian Church felt it needed to respond to new views of material reality. By the

16th Century, the Church had adopted and wedded itself to the specifics of the Three-Story Universe model of creation rather than to the basic understanding of the reality and process of Creation described above. This attachment to the TSU caused the Church to be threatened by the idea that the moon isn't a disk on the dome of the sky, but is a round rock; or the idea that the earth isn't in the center of the universe but is another rock orbiting the sun; or, much later, the notion that the earth is very old and the form of creatures changed over time.

This feeling of threat and fear was the beginning of at least 300 years of split and conflict between science and faith and it's important to understand what's at the heart of this conflict and sense of threat. When the Church became attached to a specific image of reality - the TSU - it boxed itself into a corner and became the author of its own woes. The TSU is the equivalent of a map. It's a picture of a certain territory. But it's not the territory itself. Just as maps change over time as we come to know more about the territory, or have new technology to view the territory, so too our images of the universe were bound to change over time. If we cling to our maps, we forget that we're interested in the territory, which always is different from the map. The TSU isn't the universe. By insisting that the TSU map was the universe, the Church helped create the conflicts we still see today.

In truth people of faith aren't fundamentally concerned with whether the earth is flat or round. From a faith perspective it makes no difference. Any arguments about science and faith ultimately revolve around the issue of whether or not there is this person called God in the Creation equation. When the Three-Story Universe falls apart because we come to have a different view of the cosmos, the biggest problem from a faith perspective is: Where does God go if

'He' isn't walking around above the dome in the sky? This is what did, and continues, to cause all of the turmoil and so we need to examine this particular issue.

When humanity began to inquire and reflect theologically, and practically, upon the creation of the earth we made two assumptions. The first assumption pushed science in a problematic direction, the second has caused countless difficulties for religion.

As Creation theology developed, we consciously and unconsciously compared the universe, as a created thing, to one of our created things. This was our first assumption. During the early years of what we now think of as modern science, the most famous of these items was a watch, one of the most complex machines of the time. People would talk about the universe as a giant watch and God, if God even exists, was the cosmic watch maker. This was fine up to a point, but the analogy created, I believe unintentionally, a very serious problem that haunts science to this day. When we saw Creation - the universe - as analogous to one of our creations, we made the whole of reality inanimate; even when we were talking about life!

As science viewed the world little watches began appearing everywhere. What science forgot was that our understanding of reality began with the observation that we had a mind to observe reality! By the time we reached the 20th century all we saw were atoms and molecules humming away according to the laws of chemistry and physics. Everything was a Newtonian machine and scientists actually had come to believe that our minds - the thing that was figuring this all out - were an accidental by-product of the work of these machines! Incredibly, most scientists, even if they don't know it, still think about the universe this way. However an analogy is an analogy: just because something is *like* something, doesn't mean it *is* that thing. The universe is like one of our creations, but it's not one of our creations.

The second problematic assumption that our Creation story made was similar to the first in that we made an analogy that we began to mistake for the real thing. When we said that God had a mind like ours, only better, we then made the analogy that God must also be like us in having a body and a location in space. You can even see this God painted on the ceiling of the Sistine chapel! So if God is a male person in space, then 'He' needs to be somewhere, and when the space above the dome in the sky disappears, then so does God. Again, however, the problem isn't that God disappeared, it's that we took our analogy too seriously; even when it broke down completely and proved to be wrong.

The so called clash between science and faith can, in many ways, be traced to these two incorrect assumptions: the Universe as a machine, and God as a material being. The first one pushed science in the direction of atheism and the second caused the Church and people of faith to become anxious and defensive. Working together, these two incorrect assumptions have created the illusion that somehow the doctrine of Creation may somehow be fundamentally incorrect; that even though we observe and experience a Creation, perhaps we are just living in a big watch that is mindlessly humming along. Not only does this make no sense to us from a faith perspective, but interestingly enough it is making less and less sense from a scientific perspective as well.

In the early to mid-twentieth century a group of physicists working on the physics of atomic and sub atomic particles made some very strange discoveries. This branch of physics, which is now known as quantum mechanics, has yielded a lot of useful and practical information about the world.[4] The results of this work have also called into question the notion that the universe is just a conglomeration of machines, running independently of mind.

Perhaps the most significant of their discoveries, at least for the purposes of this conversation, is that the act of observation itself helps create reality. What does this mean? The assumption of the 'world as clock' view is that material reality exists independently of anyone observing it. Again, using the analogy of one of our creations, just as we assume that once we make something and put it in the closet it is there until we take it out, so too anything in reality exists in a certain form whether we see it or not. However, this apparently isn't quite the way things are.

Physics experiments have revealed that until particles are observed, they actually exist in all possible states. Thus, as a very simple example, if we want to look for a sub atomic particle in a room, we can find it. However, before we look, the particle isn't just in one place in the room waiting to be found, rather it is *everywhere* in the room at the same time. Then when we look for it, the particle appears in one specific

---

[4] In each chapter I will describe various scientific conclusions and discoveries. As this isn't a scientific paper, I am not going to give direct references for such conclusions, although I have used these original sources in developing this work. I will indicate whether discoveries and conclusions are generally agreed upon by the majority of the scientific community or whether they are speculations or unproved. The original works of quantum physics, biochemistry, cell biology, etc. are largely unreadable by the general public. There are many works that describe these fields for the layperson and I would encourage anyone who's interested to consult these works. If you read in these fields I believe that you will see that I've done a reasonably good job of being faithful to the rubric of 'proven' and 'unproven' scientific claims.

place. This is very strange, but what these results imply is simply that our minds interact with reality to help create our world. Such a result is in sharp and direct contradiction to the prevailing modern view that the world is creating itself without any help from consciousness.

The first step in the non-TSU view of reality is to shed the two assumptions about Creation that have limited people of faith as they try to faithfully describe material reality.

First, the Creation isn't an inanimate object like one of our watches. That was the view of an earlier age of science, and it's still a pretty good approximation of how things work on the level of large things like planets and trains and other macroscopic items. However, it appears that on a more fundamental level of reality, a universe that exists must be in relationship with a mind that creates.

Secondly, whereas the Creator must have a mind in order to create, God doesn't need the spatial properties of embodied human beings in order to exist. God isn't occupying space up in the sky, walking around on a dome.

When we allow ourselves to discard these two assumptions about both God and Creation, then we begin to see the possibility of a God who is in fact the God of Creation. However, our faithful understanding of our world isn't just about Creation as a static or one-time event. We also claim that our world is 'in-Spirited'; God isn't just the One who made the universe and then left it alone, God also inhabits and influences our world. We now turn our attention to this aspect of reality.

Chapter 2

Inspirited Creation
(Incarnation/Holy Spirit)

Life is surprisingly hard to define. It is both elusive and easy to take for granted. As a result we can easily treat living beings as machines and forget this quality of life altogether.

How do we know that something is alive? This is a challenging question. Life is one of those things that is very easy for us to spot, but very difficult to pin down in a formal definition. Hundreds of books have been written on this subject and I'm not going to review all of this information here. Rather, I want to point out a few very important qualities of living things that are valuable for our understanding of reality.

Living things have the ability to organize large amounts of information and energy. Over time they use this energy and information to act in the world - they keep going! A rock, or any other inanimate object, doesn't do this. A rock may keep existing, but it doesn't use energy or information to act in the world - it just sits there. Clouds may use a lot of energy and their storms may act upon us, but eventually they disappear. The cloud couldn't keep going and acting in the world because clouds don't use energy in a manner that is self-sustaining. There was action, but no ongoing organization of information.

Living systems are organized into very small units that we call cells. It is noteworthy that all creatures, except for viruses which don't meet many of the criteria for living beings, are organized this way. We are not just one big blob, but rather we are made up of billions of very small, well-defined blobs. What's the significance of this type of organization?

At very small scales, we are dealing with atoms and molecules, and this has some interesting and important implications for how life can exist.

The first implication is that the large and small molecules that comprise cells can move through them utilizing just the heat energy of the cellular system itself. That is, there is almost zero mechanical energy required to move the cellular material around. While this may not sound like a big deal, it means that the energy used by the cell is not used for mechanical energy, but rather is used to organize the cellular components in the manner needed to keep the cell running. The energy is used to form the cells themselves.

Molecules that move under the influence of heat move randomly. They wander around. Obviously if every molecule in our body just wandered randomly, we would fall apart. Our cells make use of this random motion to allow the cellular components to move through the cell, but the random motion is also constrained and organized such that complete chaos doesn't break out.

The second implication of the tiny size is that cellular mechanisms often operate on a level of size and function where the effects of quantum mechanics that I discussed in the previous chapter begin to come into play. If you look in biology text books you will see pictures that claim to be models of the molecules that make up our cells: proteins, carbohydrates, fats, and the stuff of our genetic material, DNA. These pictures represent these molecules in ball and stick figures. The balls are the atoms and the sticks are the bonds between them. However we know that this picture is a highly inaccurate approximation of reality.

What might be more accurate is to show a model that was a movie of a cloud, a haze in which the atoms might be someplace, but also might be somewhere else. From the point of view of our knowledge of these very small systems, it is important to ask: what is it that makes our cells 'real' and 'stable' and continue to function such that they make up a living part of our body? We are back to the question of what makes them alive?

The doctrine of Creation isn't just about the initial creation of the universe. Many passages in Scripture describe the role God has in upholding creation, in making creatures come and go. God has a role in the living and dying process. Theologically we claim that God is *continuously* creating, God upholds the universe and makes it stable.

This aspect of Creation is almost impossible to understand or make sense of within a TSU model of reality. If God is a creature in space, up above the clouds somewhere, how can such a creature possibly maintain the creation? How can an old guy in the sky maintain life? Such a role has often been assigned to the Holy Spirit. The Spirit, or breath of God, is the person of God that is somehow involved in the continuing aspect of creation. We can relate to this concept because breath and spirit are invisible and fluid. We can imagine such an entity traveling down from the heavens and invisibly influencing the earth in some way, just as the wind messes up our hair on a windy day.

Yet this image is still quite problematic because of the specific qualities of life. The wind is inanimate. It cannot maintain and organize information over time. We describe the Holy Spirit as a person. Yet within the modern Scientific view of reality, it has been very hard to understand how a person, which we think of as existing in material space, might exist to influence life on earth. However, if our understanding of God is non-spatial; if God is simply the 'mind in reality that creates' then we have many other options at our disposal for understanding how God can influence our earth (I will take up a more detailed discussion of God in chapter 4).

One possible conclusion, given our understanding of microscopic reality, is that living creatures exist as stable and ongoing entities because there is a mind continually observing them and thinking them into existence. This conclusion is consistent with the observations about organization, energy, and information discussed above.

Furthermore these living beings, by virtue of being living, are participating in that same mind. Thus all of our Creation not only has been brought into being by the mind we call God, but furthermore the ongoing creation and existence of life is maintained by a continual creation that is also inspirited by the mind of God.

This is a dramatic conclusion and not 'proven' scientifically at this time. However, it is a possible conclusion given our current understanding of material reality, and it is one that is potentially testable. Furthermore, it certainly is a conclusion that can't be completely ruled out or dismissed simply because someone doesn't like the possibility.

If true, how might we understand this assertion, and how might we understand the action of God in a world that is inhabited by the Holy Spirit? I'll begin with an analogy from the macroscopic world of our creations as an example of what a world filled with Spirit implies about living beings.

Say we want to create a house. In order to do this, we must spend a lot of time thinking about that house. We plan, we make drawings, we shape materials in certain ways, we bring together bits of matter and place them in an ordered fashion with other bits of matter. We communicate with other people and involve them in the process to help us. All of this thinking is of primary importance in order to make the house come into being. The house doesn't create itself, and our thinking isn't just a funny by-product of the creation of the house.

At the end of the process we have a house. It's done. It functions in certain ways. Some of those functions may even be automatic, for example the septic tank might empty itself when it gets full. However, we wouldn't say that the house is alive. It cannot organize information over time and act in the world. Up to this point, we have the analogy of the first creation. We have played God and created the world of our house.

Now what would have to happen in order for our house to be alive? For our house to live, it would have to have some of the same qualities that we have. It would have to be able to perform some of the same functions that our thinking and creating performed to make it in the first place. If a shingle came off the roof, the house would notice and would have some way to go to the store and get another shingle. As the house got older, it would have some way to make another baby house. In short, it would be able to participate in creation and in order to do this it would have to have some of the qualities of mind because mind is the primary creator of our reality.

Should our house 'come to life' we would now have a situation analogous to the world once human beings appeared in creation. Before the house got it's own mind, the only mind present was ours, God's. Now both God's mind (us) and the creature's mind (the house) exist in the same space. Both the house and ourselves begin to work together on our creation, the house, and we can imagine how this situation unfolds. We want to paint the house brown, but the house prefers steel siding. We want large windows in the living room, but the house prefers small windows. Sometimes the house listens to us, sometimes it doesn't. Our mind, like the Spirit of God, is continuously present in creation but isn't the only actor on the scene.

This analogy can aid the discussion about the Spirit of God being continuously present in upholding and forming of creation; a topic that in turn leads us into one of the most challenging areas of practical theology, namely how it is that God works in the world. This issue is framed and discussed in many different ways. Some of the variations include questions about whether God micromanages every event, or whether God is responsible for every bad disaster or act, or whether we have free will if God is acting in reality. These are important issues and I will touch upon them in different ways throughout this work; here I begin the conversation with reflections upon how observation and thought interact with matter.

When we perform experiments on subatomic particles, we observe them. Before the observations the particles exist not as solid objects, but rather as potentials of many states of being. Yet once we observe them, they assume a certain state of existence and then act in accordance with that state. Thus the particle moves from a condition of almost infinite potential to a condition of having an observable path of existence.

Once this change from potential to actual occurs, a shift that is even called the 'collapse of the wave function,' we find that the particle now begins to act, at least for a while, more like a solid macroscopic object. In such a state, particles may even have this collapsing effect on one another, and there are those who wish to claim, although this is unproven, that the particles 'measure' each other in the absence of an observing mind.

These observations give a picture of a world that is moving in and out of potentiality. In one condition, there are lots of possibilities. Then that potential is lost for a while before another open moment occurs some time later. The change from potentiality to actuality is conditioned by observation and measurement; and we even have evidence that this change can occur at great distances if particles have interacted at some time in the past. This picture of reality is far more fluid and strange than how we usually consider the universe but it's not completely unfamiliar.

Consider the process that anyone goes through who wishes to bring a new idea into fruition in the world. When we are mulling over our idea it can become well formed, perfectly clear in our minds. We might visualize the product of our idea, and see how we can create this product. Or our idea creates a new situation that seems obviously valuable and helpful, and we know that everyone will agree that we've come up with an excellent plan. Then we try and implement our idea.

Anyone who has tried an entrepreneurial venture knows what happens next. We encounter all sorts of issues, obstacles, and problems. The perfect vision that we had in our head becomes much less perfect. The materials we thought we'd use for our new product don't work as we thought, and there isn't a machine that can handle the material properly. Then hardly anyone likes our idea, or at least they are highly skeptical. Other problems arise with those who are helping us; they don't quite understand how to put the new idea into practice, or they have their own modifications to our idea that may or may not work so well.

As our idea moves from the potential to the actual things don't go the way we thought they would. Even though we could imagine how our idea would manifest, when we implement our plan we encounter all of the other ideas and realities in the world. Our new idea has to bump into these realities and try to fit into a world that is already full of activity. Although our new concept may be fantastic, it cannot appear fully formed in the material world, but rather it must find a way to move into a world that is quite solid and set in its ways. This is the process of moving from potentiality to actuality, and it happens in the macroscopic world just as in the microscopic world.

We are told that in the heavenly realms God's will is done perfectly. It's on earth that there is a problem. When God wishes to act in material existence, the Spirit of God encounters the same movement from potential to actual that we do. How else can we explain the fact that God's will isn't done on earth? God does have thoughts for the best, and may have the best thoughts, yet these plans must find their way through the competing muck of the material world which is full of actual events and activity, as well as the competing thoughts of our minds. No wonder salvation history unfolds so slowly!

Therefore anything that happens is determined by multiple causes, one of which is the upholding creative thought of God. This doesn't mean that God has no power or doesn't act. Rather it means that in the material world, God's actions, the new things that God is doing, come into the world through the same process of potential moving to actual as any other new creative thought. Of course God has more of these, and the greater power of God comes about because of the immensity of God's mind, the topic of a later chapter.

The action of the Holy Spirit in the world is thus not an action that micromanages or directly causes every event. In a material world with billions of minds at work this would be impossible. Rather the Spirit is the mind that is always present, bringing the best, most loving, most hopeful thought into the midst of every situation.

It is ironic that people who wish to deny the existence of God talk about the creation of the universe and our world as being 'random' or 'chance'. It is ironic because from what we now know scientifically, the exact opposite is true. Randomness is the nature and state of atoms and other particles when there is no mind to observe them. In this state they do not exist in an ordered fashion but rather in some statistical never never land where nothing is stable or ordered. If our universe was truly random, it wouldn't exist at all.

The fact that there is a stable configuration of reality means that there is also a mind that is observing that reality, and further more it is observing it in a particular way. In physics this principle of the uniqueness of our creation has come to be called the anthropic principle, and this concept is remarkably similar to what our faith stories and theology tell us. How we as observers ask questions determines what we see and come to know. If our world is a continuing creation that supports life then there must be a mind looking for a life-supporting reality. As Isaiah says, God chose us.

From this point we can now ask more particular questions about human beings and what it means to 'share' in the mind of God. The next chapter takes up the issue of theological anthropology in a non Three-Story Universe.

Chapter 3

Human Beings:
A Theological Anthropology

People are the beings who reflect upon God and the universe. We are not aware of another creature engaging in such reflection. In the first chapter I pointed out that as living beings with awareness we occupy a particular place in the created order. Awareness allows for the possibility of dominion over the world. We are able to make choices and influence the environment in ways no other living entity can. This observation says nothing about *how* we should interact with the environment or what are the nature and quality of our choices. So far I have simply made the observation that when we wake up in the morning we find ourselves in possession of this capacity.

Our faith tradition, our scripture, and our theology, are concerned with the position of humanity in the created order. This is fitting, given that we are the ones who are making the observations about God and the world. In the Three-Story Universe model of reality, people are created by God and plunked down on the face of the earth. Furthermore, the claim is made that we are created in the 'image of God.' Ironically, we can blame this phrase for our own popular image of God: since God created us in their own image, we have returned the favor! If we are physical bipedal humans, then, as I mentioned above, we think God must be one as well.

There are some Christians I've talked to who wish to deny that this popular TSU model of God is operative in the consciousness of most believers. However, as I mentioned in the introduction, this denial is attributable to the invisible nature of the common image. Two recent examples point out this difficulty. The first was a sermon I heard at a Presbyterian Seminary given by a student in his twenties. I'm sure this young man would identify himself as a postmodern believer, someone in tune with all the current church trends. Yet at one point in his sermon, without any hesitancy or sense of the absurdity of the phrase, he referred to God as 'the big guy upstairs,' an image that derives directly from the TSU.

In the second example, a pastor from a large church dismissed my idea that the TSU was an important and enduring Christian image of God and reality. His church population is sophisticated and educated, and he thought that such notions were no longer operating in his community. The day after we had our initial conversation, he told me that he had to rethink his ideas. When he arrived home the night after stating his opinion about the TSU, he had a conversation with a bright young man who was a friend of his son and another educated postmodern person. The young man asked him if the Church still thought of God as an old man in the sky; the implication of the question being that the young adult felt this was the image the Church taught. The pastor told me that in light of this conversation he needed to rethink his ideas about the TSU. We all need to do this rethinking because as the Hubble telescope continues to fail at finding the old guy in the heavenly throne, it becomes clear we need to reconfigure how we understand both God and ourselves.

The previous chapter brought us to the point of understanding living creation as entities participating in the mind of God. As mind creates it leaves a trace of its actions within the beings of living creatures and thus animates them.

They live because they are inspirited.   There is someone thinking them into being.

However there is more to this story.   Not all living creatures manifest the same quality of mind.   Bacteria, viruses, and plants have no discernible brains or nervous systems.   In the animal realm we see a wide variety of nervous systems that control their host's actions and functions to varying degrees.   People have a brain that has been described as the most complex machine in the known universe.   The mind of God may be holding all of these different creatures in living states, but life comes in different forms, and the capacity of mind manifests differently in each creature.   At the same time we know, as I stated above, that all this life is interconnected and interrelated.

As life appears upon the earth, the process of Creation has seen a parade of living beings moving towards a being with the capacity to enflesh a fully aware mind. Life on earth exhibits a tremendous range of ability.   In every creature the Spirit of God moves and breaths and experiences some particular quality of embodied life. All of this is good. And none of the creatures, except us, can see the whole picture. They are not self aware.

Once humanity appeared on earth, a creature developed that could describe and depict the Creation. What a delight! Several years ago I was at an exhibit of the history of ancient Greek art.   The earliest pieces of art in this exhibit were about 5500 years old and the later pieces were 2000 years old.   The change in art forms from the earliest pieces to the latest pieces was fascinating.   The early pieces showed very basic shapes and colors of people and animals. The faces had little detail; the animals were like stick figures.   They were similar to the cave paintings that many of us have seen. By contrast, the later pieces were the incredibly detailed paintings and pottery that often define ancient Greek art. Moving through the exhibit and observing these changes, one could watch the human mind becoming clearer, more able to understand, process, and depict its environment; in the mirror of the art you could see the human mind coming into existence. Looking at art from any culture around the world would yield the same result. In the period from 5000-500BC there is a radical change in the human minds' ability to observe and reflect its surroundings; and in this change we see the final evolution of mind breaking fully into the material realm.

When this happened, both the mind of God, and the human mind became present simultaneously on earth. Two aware minds now exist on the material plane of reality. This observation helps us understand the theological assertion that we are formed in God's image: we can see and create and know in ways that are similar to the way God can see and create and know. It is no coincidence that the change in the human mind seen in the artistic record corresponds roughly with the Biblical time frame of the garden of Eden story.

When certain people of faith wish to talk about a 'young earth' and say that the earth is only 6000 years old, what they are really saying, although most would never admit this, is that humanity's awareness and knowledge of the earth is 6000 years old. This is in fact true (to a rough approximation of several thousand years)! Before that, the only actively aware mind in the universe was the mind of God, and from God's perspective time looks very different (I will say more about this in the next chapter).

Using these observations about a creation that has become increasingly mindful; let's now think more about the two most basic theological issues regarding human beings:

that we are created in God's image, and that we have 'fallen' into a world or a condition of sin.

As I mentioned at the beginning of the chapter, the scriptural assertion that we are created in God's image has been popularly translated to mean that God looks like us! All of the great artistic renderings in cathedrals and paintings have tended to show God in human male form. This tendency has been exacerbated by the fact that Jesus was a human male and we consider him to be 'fully God.' Even when theologians and preachers have insisted that God isn't an embodied man, popular images and discussions continue to reinforce this idea; it is so engrained in the minds of large numbers of Christians that recent efforts to use feminine pronouns and non-male images for God have often met with violent resistance.

Within the Three-Story Universe model of reality, this projection of ourselves upon God is both natural and understandable. God was seen to be a bigger, stronger, heavenly version of ourselves, striding around on the dome above the sky. Other ancient near eastern religions had similar visions of the gods: people, only bigger!

Of course, no such big people have been found in outer space and thus we require another view. From what we now understand about the nature of reality we can say that a mind that is aware and can organize reality, i.e. create, is an 'image' of God that fits what we know about the universe (I will have more to say about this in the next chapter). This is exactly what we know ourselves to be!

As soon as human beings were aware of the contents of their environment, they began to draw them on the walls of caves. Our minds, once they came into existence, began to create. We fashioned tools and shelters and clothes and art. The creative impulse is so strong in us it would be hard to imagine being a person and *not* creating something, anything. Therefore, rather than understanding our particular physical embodiment as being the image of God in which we are made, we should understand that term to mean that as aware beings that create we are made in the image of *the* being that creates not only us, but the entire universe. This is how we are made in God's image.

One clue that this impulse to create is how we should understand being created in God's image is that humanity so often philosophizes about why we create. We are obsessed with this subject, and yet we fail to find a simple human answer as to why it is such a fundamental part of our being! In 1968 someone even made a movie called "Why Man Creates." Within certain artistic circles people discuss, often with some sarcasm or disdain because they know they'll never fully arrive at an answer, the question "What is art?" This creative impulse is so deeply rooted and fundamental that it almost escapes description and conceptualization. The image of God would be such a fundamental aspect of our being.

Before continuing on to a discussion of the Fall, I want to explain why I'm not using 'soul' as part of my description of the human person, but rather am relying more on the 'mind' as the aspect of our being that relates more directly with the non-material or spiritual world. Historically the soul has been described as that part of ourselves fashioned by God before we were conceived and then placed in our material bodies. In popular faith and culture our soul is then released from the body after death and continues into the afterlife.

Such a description posits the soul as a thing, an entity of some sort. By contrast, mind is not a thing or entity, but rather is a process, the process of organizing and making sense of reality. The content of mind are thoughts and thoughts aren't solid but rather are a flow of perceptions, ideas, and mental constructs or images.

If the soul is a thing we must address the question of where and what is it as it inhabits the body. People have engaged in such a search by, for example, weighing bodies immediately after death to determine if the soul has weight. Nothing useful has come from such measurements.

The idea of soul as a thing has also created many problems when trying to theologically understand what is happening with identical twins, or embryos that die long before birth, or with various strange genetic mutations that produce babies with parts from different embryos. If in each of these conditions a fully formed soul was put into a single celled fertilized human egg, then either God wastes a lot of souls or perhaps we need to question the usefulness of a concept that fits so poorly with what we now know about humanity.

If there is no evidence for a thing called a soul, and we cannot find it or describe it, then either it doesn't exist, or it at least isn't useful in any description of our material reality that connects with a scientific view of that same reality. On the other hand our minds exist. Furthermore, asserting that mind is a process and not a thing is congruent with both our personal experience of reality, and our scientific experience of our brains. When we open a brain we can't find a mind! It's not a substance but a process that occurs within a fully formed human brain.

It's because of these very distinct, important differences between the mind and the soul that I am using one and not the other. Of course, if one wants to understand the soul as our unique pattern of mind, then the two terms can be seen as interchangeable.

The Fall is a theological doctrine that has come under much attack and scrutiny within the American Church over the past 30 years. There are many churches and Christians that don't even like mentioning it, and often these groups don't want to talk about sin any more either. Perhaps this is a reflection of our recent desire to create 'good self-esteem' in everyone, and people feel that if they regard themselves and others as fallen then they won't have a good self image. I personally find this analysis and concern unconvincing and even ridiculous (in much the same way that I think it's ridiculous to give almost every child an 'A' no matter how bad their work, a common occurrence in many modern American schools). One only has to read the papers or get to know your community to understand that the world we live in has enough problems, evil, and general bad behavior to call it 'fallen'. If what we inhabit is a world without sin, I'd never want to live in a world *with* sin!

However, there is a more significant issue with the doctrine of the Fall given that our understanding of this doctrine comes out of the TSU model. Traditionally, our concept of sin and Fall comes from the Garden of Eden story. Although at first glance this story may not seem directly related to the TSU, they are connected because the creation model on display in Genesis 2 and 3 is dependent on the TSU. God is up in the sky, creating upon the flat disk, creation comes about whole and fully formed, and seemingly 'perfect', then things go downhill from there.

As with everything else about the TSU, we now know that this image of creation is simply not true, literally speaking. Science claims that there was no 'perfect' place of fully formed creation. Rather science reveals that creatures and the universe in general have evolved over time; and history tells us that we aren't getting any better or worse from a moral point of view. We would be hard pressed to say if a cow is any more or less perfect then a dinosaur; and there wasn't a time when human beings were morally more or less better than we are now.   So if the Fall is a valid theological proposition, what can it possibly mean within a new model of reality?

We begin to answer this question by looking at the Garden of Eden story itself and asking, "What would we say about an adult person who didn't know that they were naked?" In our current day and age we might describe such a person as developmentally disabled or delayed.   We certainly would think that they had a problem and we wouldn't recognize such a person as being 'normal.'   This person couldn't function in modern day society.   They couldn't learn, couldn't hold a job, couldn't feed or take care of themselves. They would be seriously handicapped. In fact such people do exist and they need significant amounts of care for their entire lives;   we certainly don't think of such people as 'perfect.'   Yet Adam and Eve are described as having exactly this limited state of awareness before the Fall.

In terms of the human person, the Garden of Eden story is about the transition from a state of non-awareness to a state of awareness. The human beings come to 'know' their surroundings, and themselves. This transition initiates the curses that are now associated with the Fall.   The state of 'perfection' that Christians associate with the Garden pre-Fall, is simply the state of creation before a fully formed human mind came into existence.   In such a state all creatures mindlessly do what they are programmed to do by their genetics in response to their environment. All such creatures are unaware that they are naked; in fact they are unaware of everything! What is 'perfect' about such a state is that the only aware mind in this situation is God's mind.   There are no other aware minds, or separate egos, to compete for attention or power or supremacy. Such a state is exactly how the world was before modern homo sapiens arrived on the scene; and it is perfect in the sense that it is undisturbed by the human drive for control over the Creation. If we look at some people's desire to preserve nature and keep wild places 'unspoiled,' we can see that they are using, perhaps unconsciously, this definition of perfection. They assert that the natural world, undisturbed by humanity is the best world, the perfect world.

Once separate aware human minds appear everything changes. Our minds develop independent egos that allow us to negotiate our world. Without them we wouldn't survive or be able to create modern human society. However the existence of the ego is also the cause of the problems in our world. When we experience ourselves as independent creatures, we become highly invested in this separate self which we now know can also not exist, or die.

This state of self awareness in the midst of the world is the source of both our will to power and control and the existential anxiety driving us to avoid death. We think if we have more food and more money and more power then we can stave off death and live a better life. Furthermore, the awareness and creation of a separate self allows for the illusion that we are the source of our life and the power to create. Our ego becomes the center of the universe and usurps the position of God in our lives.

Just as in the Biblical story, the creation of an aware human mind is both the beginning of human society, the need for and ability to work, and the beginning of sin and a human understanding of death. Awareness, human creation, and the Fall are coexistent. As we realize this truth, we can re-orient our TSU description of humanity knowing that indeed we are formed in the image of God, yet are also living within a Fallen world. Having claimed a robust understanding of both of these theological claims outside of the TSU we can now turn our attention to a description of God in the modern universe.

Chapter 4

God

It's hard to fit God into a universe governed by scientific theory and observation. The resistance and violent opposition from the Church and Christians to various scientific views and descriptions of material reality are the result of this difficulty. As soon as the dome over the sky was pulled back to reveal the seemingly empty vacuum of space, God was in big trouble. In fact the old Soviet propaganda machine even tried to use this fact of empty space to support its atheist agenda. They claimed that one of its early cosmonauts said that he went into space and God wasn't there, and thus couldn't exist. Where did He (sic) go and was He (sic) ever there to begin with?

Time also became a problem. When the created universe was small and new the whole spiritual enterprise was manageable. However, once the universe became both vast and very old, then God was pushed to the margins of space and also to the margins of time. God became far away and too old. Finally, as we discovered the various scientific laws that govern reality, it seemed there was no longer the need for an intelligent agent to make things go. Now God was out of real estate, out of time, and out of a job. At this point, God just went 'poof' and vanished all together. What is a faithful response to these concerns?

Just as I began this work with the earth, because that is where we find ourselves when we wake up in the morning, I begin a discussion of God with us, and our experience, because we are the ones who talk about God. Observing human theological reflection, we notice several interesting aspects to our speech about God.

First, all people throughout history have had some religious or spiritual impulse and describe some 'other' at work in the universe. I would include in this list scientific atheists for whom the 'other' are the 'laws of nature,' an independent, self-existent other that controls reality.

Some have taken this observation about the universal nature of religious thought, and concluded that humanity is just suffering from a massive delusion. However I think this is an unscientific conclusion and it ignores the evidence of human history and anthropology. If indeed God, and our theological impulse, a desire to seek the One who created and seeks us, is not real, then we would expect at least one culture or society or group of people who would be true atheists; they would have no longing for or interest in God. But there's no such thing. Even those who claim to be atheists are often the most obsessed with God and talk about God more than people of faith. I would suggest that the universality of the 'other' is a piece of evidence that God exists.

The second thing we notice about people and God is that God is discussed and conceived through the use of our minds. This is an obvious but important statement. Animals don't worry about God. They have no altars, no behavior that indicates they are concerned about a deity. This is because they don't have a mind that can conceive of or communicate with God.

When we look at the response of many people to the abandonment of the TSU, we can see how important it is to recognize that the search for God occurs via the human mind. Rather than abandon God, many have turned to contemplative religions like Buddhism and Hinduism to express their faith because in these systems of faith, the mind, rather than story or doctrine, is the center of the practice of faith. Another alternative has been New Age 'religion.' This isn't any one system of faith but rather a loose affiliation of beliefs that borrows from many faiths. The one concept common within most New Age circles is the notion that people can become 'God-like' through an evolved use of the mind. In the absence of a spatial and temporal God our minds again become the center of our faith practice.

Within the Christian faith, meditation and contemplative practices have also been an essential component of deep faith. There is a rich tradition describing the experience of union with God which occurs either in a mind trained in contemplative practice, or as a spontaneous revelation of God into the mind of the believer. If our aware mind is what distinguishes us as being formed in God's image, then it's not surprising that our mind is what allows us to talk about, think about, long for, and describe God.

These two observations about humanity in relation to God also allow us to speak theologically about God in a scientific universe because they give us a glimpse of a new way of understanding God in a non-TSU.

At the beginning of the chapter I identified three issues, or problems, related to God and the modern universe. They were: space, time, and action. When we look at these three categories of description, we can see that the problem we have with God outside of the TSU is the same problem we had with people and the image of God question: if we define God in terms that reflect our own condition then we are going to run into difficulty. So just as there was a problem with imagining God as a bodily being when we considered how we are formed in God's image, in the same way if we define God in terms of space and time and physical work, because that's how we experience life, we will ultimately see that this is an inadequate way to consider God's existence.

One of the most interesting scientific discoveries of the 20th century was an understanding of action at a distance. This discovery, which has been called Bell's theorem, recognized that once two sub-atomic particles were 'entangled,' that is had interacted with each other, then they could effect one another's properties instantaneously at a distance. This action at a distance sounds like science fiction to us who are trapped inside of space and time. However this property of the universe has received experimental validation and it gives a physical correlate to what most people have experienced in terms of 'knowing' certain things instantly and at a distance.

Although there continues to be a great deal of debate and skepticism about what has been commonly labeled 'ESP,' or extra-sensory perception (a very poor name for a number of reasons), most humans have had the experience of knowing something before it was communicated to them through 'normal' time/space channels. Even though our modern culture, which is trapped in a materialistic view of reality, tells us that such knowledge is either wrong or somehow a fantasy, there are mountains of anecdotal evidence to show that such knowledge occurs.

One brief, but very significant, example comes from the experiences of a pastor who was assigned to teach communications at a college in Australia. The college enrollment consisted predominantly of aboriginal students and the pastor soon found out that these young people knew far more about human communication technology than he did. He regularly observed them transmitting news at the college to their home communities instantaneously with no direct 'normal' communication techniques. He had no idea how this occurred but was told by his students that it was normal for their culture and that such communication took place via the 'dreamtime.'

What these experiences, and Bell's theorem, point to is that information can, and does, transcend our common boundaries of time and space. Science and experience have come to confirm what mystics have known and discussed for thousands of years; namely that mind is a property of reality that isn't dependent on what we call time or space. While this may sound abstract or irrelevant, it is a very important observation and leads us to a vision of what God looks like in the modern era: God is the mind of the universe that is independent of time and space. Furthermore the action of such a mind occurs not through force acting on a mass (this is the way we do things) but rather through thought forming and stabilizing matter itself (as discussed in chapter 1).

This understanding of God as disembodied mind actually makes perfect sense from a scriptural, and practical, point of view. If God could indeed create the universe, at which point time and space were also created, then God would have to exist as a mind 'prior' (although not in the sense of past time), or outside, these events. Such a being could not be constrained by either time or space. The action of such a being is best described by something like 'speaking.' God as disembodied Word is a much better image for God then some old guy walking around on top of the sky (although such an image doesn't do much for Michelangelo!). It wasn't until the incarnation that God as Word took on or entered into the constraints of our time and space (more on this in the next chapter).

At this point it's appropriate to say more about the issue of evidence and proof in relation to God and all things spiritual. For many people in the modern world, this is an important issue as well as a common argument for those who wish to claim that God doesn't exist. These people feel, or assert, that there is no 'evidence' of God's existence or that you can't 'prove' that God exits. As I hinted at above, I think this claim is inaccurate but it's an important issue to address directly.

To begin with, we have to realize, and admit, that most of what we take for scientific evidence is just someone else's report of scientific evidence. The vast majority of people have never seen, nor could they understand, the actual evidence for the majority of things that we take for granted are 'true.' We think that there is evidence for the existence of the atom, for example, but we couldn't read the results of a bubble chamber experiment, or a particle accelerator experiment, or any other such results. The average person would be unable to evaluate the conclusions in almost any scientific journal article. When we *believe* a set of scientific conclusions we accept *on faith* that these documents include evidence for the conclusions they claim are true.

Because we accept scientific conclusions on faith, what the average person doesn't perhaps realize is that claims of evidence and truth in scientific exploration are much more vague and conditional than we are normally led to believe. Corporations regularly exploit this ignorance and make 'scientific' claims in product ads that are completely false. However they know that the public has no way to evaluate and discover these lies. Once we realize this faith component to our understanding of scientific evidence, we begin to see that in some ways our relationship to science is much like a religion: we have faith in something that we barely understand, but we believe in the experts to whom we give authority to mediate truth for us.

We also give these experts the authority to tell us those things for which there is *no* evidence. Most people who claim to be atheists or agnostics will tell you that there is 'no evidence' for the existence of God. What they mean by this statement is that they have been told by a scientist that there is no evidence for the existence of God and that they are taking the claims of this scientist on faith and believe them to be true.

Does this claim of no evidence have any validity? In order to answer this question we need to first discuss the nature of evidence in science. Science is simply a process for exploring reality. This process has several basic steps: a question, or hypothesis, is asked; an experiment or set of observations is designed to address this question; the experiment is conducted many times; the results of the observation, known as evidence, are gathered and evaluated relative to the question, and a conclusion is reached relative to the hypothesis.

In order for this process to work, for truth to be discovered, two things are necessary. The set of observations must be appropriate for the question, and the experiment must be repeatable by others so that individual bias or deception can be avoided, or at least minimized. This last requirement is very important and it is the repeatable nature of experimentation that gives science its claim of 'objective truth,' that is without personal, subjective bias.

In recent years however, many different disciplines have discussed that true objectivity is impossible. There are two reasons for this. First, because all evidence is ultimately filtered through and evaluated by the human mind it is subject to human bias. Secondly, reality itself is created in part by observation! The questions we ask and the experiments we choose to do have a role in causing the results.

The people who claim that there is no evidence for God make this claim based on their belief that human experience cannot constitute scientific evidence because it is not 'objective.' They contrast this lack of objectivity with science which they claim is objective. However this argument is a faulty one. All evidence carries with it an element of subjectivity. Thus dismissing evidence based upon subjective experience per se isn't a valid scientific procedure. Rather the appropriate question should be: what evidence about God is appropriate evidence?

Obviously just one person saying so isn't appropriate. Nor should we even take at face value the say of many people, or any one particular organization. To determine what evidence might be appropriate, we must go back to the description of the scientific process. This process tells us that we must choose experimental methods and evidence that are appropriate to the question or hypothesis we are exploring. In relation to God, our question is whether or not there exists an independent mind within the universe, and our hypothesis is that such a mind exists. If this is the form of our question, then the appropriate method for evaluating this hypothesis is some way of examining our own minds to see if there is another mind 'out there' to communicate with.

It turns out that such methods of examination of mind exist, and have existed for thousands of years. These are the methods and practices of contemplation. Such practices are much like any other scientific methods in that they are repeatable and describable. Anyone can do them in any time and place and culture.

It turns out that people have done this experiment, millions of people! The truth is that this 'search for God' is probably the most repeated experiment in all of history; and the evidence is overwhelming. God is found with a regularity that far exceeds the success of any other scientific experiment.

What has often confused people about this conclusion is that the description of God varies tremendously from culture to culture and time to time; and I will say more about this issue in a later chapter. However remember our original hypothesis: there is an independent mind in the universe that we call God. This says nothing about doctrine or dogma or cultural or linguistic description of this mind, this God. These issues weren't part of our original hypothesis or experimental design. What humans have found, with incredible regularity and predictability is an "Other" at work in reality.

This discussion began with the question: is there any evidence for the existence of God? I would suggest that the answer is an emphatic yes: there are mountains of evidence. Of course, people are free to reject, or not believe the evidence in the same way that they could reject the evidence for any other scientific truth that we must take on faith. However, this rejection isn't an issue of evidence, it's an issue of personal belief. Furthermore, anyone is certainly welcome to design experiments to test the evidence and the hypothesis and present this evidence for evaluation. What isn't scientific however, is simply to say there is no evidence just because someone else told me so! If the same person who says this about God said this about any other theory they would be laughed out of the lab.

From the preceding discussion we see that 'science' and 'faith' are more deeply intertwined than a modern person with a scientific world view might choose to admit (certainly in more ways than those who consider themselves to be a hard-core scientific atheist would acknowledge!). As the scientific exploration of the universe reveals things about reality that conform to a surprising degree with what religious and, especially, contemplative traditions have been claiming for years, the disciplines of science and faith appear to be converging rather than diverging.   This convergence is especially powerful with the broad theological categories of God and Creation discussed above.   But what about the theological categories more particular to the Christian faith? To begin this exploration, I now turn to Jesus, the most particular aspect of all Christian theology.

Chapter 5

Jesus

Recently, someone said to me, "I'd write a scientific Christian theology, but I wouldn't know what to do with Jesus." I began the previous chapter with the claim that God doesn't easily fit into the scientific universe. It is even harder to find a place for Jesus. As with God, there are several particular problems that we encounter when we try to align our theological understandings and claims with our scientific world view.

The first is the problem of miracles and the various stories and assertions made about Jesus, his life, death, and resurrection. Events such as the virgin birth, the healing miracles, and the resurrection itself cause many people who live within the scientific world view to shudder and become skeptical. They feel if they have to accept a literal, 'scientific,' understanding of these events then they cannot accept Jesus or any other claim made about him.

The second problem arises from an evolutionary perspective. If all of life is evolving based upon certain laws and principles of natural selection, then the sudden, divinely driven, appearance of a particular special person breaks these evolutionary laws and apparently violates evolutionary principles. Furthermore, that such a person would need to appear to alleviate sin or perform some other action related to a Fall scenario is also problematic; as I discussed in chapter 3.

Finally, Jesus presents the problem of particularity: how could one person, in one time and place be the particular manifestation of God for everyone? This is a theological problem in and of itself and not just in relation to science. However this issue, and the question of the nature of other religions which arises from the particularity problem, is very important, especially in our globalized, shrinking world. Because it is so essential, and of a slightly different character than the first two problems, I defer this third issue to the final chapter.

The first two issues, that of miracles and that of Jesus in an evolutionary perspective, address the questions: who was, and is, Jesus? what did he do? and how did he do it? How can we discuss these issues from the point of view of our modern scientific understanding of reality?

These questions are made more difficult because Christianity talks about Jesus as 'the Christ.' Thus there is Jesus, the supposed human being, a historical figure from first century Palestine; and there is 'the Christ' the second person of the Trinity who is God. For some people, these are one and the same being. Other Christians tend to separate these two in their minds. I've often encountered people who don't like to use 'Jesus' and 'the Christ' as interchangeable terms because they somehow see them as different things or aspects of God, or perhaps they feel they understand one better than another. My understanding of the bulk of Christian doctrine and theology is that one cannot separate 'Jesus' from 'the Christ.' Jesus is the Word made flesh, fully God and fully human. Although other theological stances certainly exist and are possible I wish to address the question of Jesus in a scientific world from the standard orthodox position: that the person Jesus was a material manifestation of the second person of the Trinity. Given this starting point, how can we address the questions raised above?

To begin, we need to look at the relationship between science and unique events. When I described the scientific method in the previous chapter, I said that one step in the scientific process was repeating the experiment many times to acquire enough evidence to be able to confidently arrive at a conclusion about your hypothesis. This aspect of repeatability is essential to the scientific method for it assures us, through the statistical analysis of the data, that some conclusion about nature is real and stable, and not just a fluke or some misjudgment.

However this same requirement for repetition, while good in that it makes the scientific method very powerful, is highly problematic when it comes to evaluating unique events. Because you cannot, by definition, repeat unique events!

Many years ago a family friend, who is a physician, cured a young boy of a horrible incurable disease through hypnosis. He received a huge amount of publicity and fame as a result of this case. He was on the cover of major national magazines, and was inundated with requests from parents all over the world to cure their children. He was never able to replicate the cure.

There are three general ways that science responds to such unique events. The first is to ignore or dismiss them as hoaxes of one kind or another. The second is to take the stance of an agnostic and say that the scientific community cannot say much of anything about such an event but that perhaps it could be studied at a later time if and when such a thing happens again. The third is to try and study a unique event by designing experiments that are enough like the event, or that contain elements of the event, with the hope of beginning to unlock the puzzle of what happened that one special time.

The unique event that science has the most difficulty with is an event that is *both* common but also, by its inability to be repeated at will, unique. Healings are one such event. So called 'miraculous' healings are not unique events but rather are quite common. I doubt there is a single person who hasn't heard of someone having a disease and then suddenly not having that disease. This phenomenon of spontaneous healing drives science and scientists crazy because it is both common and yet cannot be controlled and repeated in an experimental situation.

Another class of events that falls into this category are what we have come to called 'psychic' events, or events related to 'spiritual powers.' As with healings, these events are common in anecdotal form but are also incredibly hard to study in the lab.

Science and scientists are particularly hostile towards such events. Perhaps this hostility is due to frustration at not being able to control or dissect these phenomena. Whatever the reason, these unique but common events are most likely to be relegated to the category of hoax (although some people try to study them or take an agnostic stance in regards to them) even though they aren't unusual.

When I went to seminary, I was quite amazed to find that most of my professors took the position that the miracle stories in the Bible weren't true, literal, descriptions of events. This position appeared to be in response to a scientific world view hostile to such events. If I had gone to a seminary that regarded itself as primarily fundamentalist, I would have found a group of professors who would insist on taking all of the stories as literal fact and would perhaps be hostile to a scientific world view. Can we approach this issue, and thus the question of Jesus from a place of integration and wholeness, even within a scientific context?

The most scientifically honest statement that can be made about the miraculous stories of Jesus is that we simply don't know what happened 2000 years ago in Palestine. This is the agnostic stance of science. Because these were unique events, they cannot be studied scientifically in the usual sense of the word. Yes, we have never seen anyone resurrected from the dead three days after they've died, but this doesn't mean it cannot happen. We now routinely raise people from the dead several minutes after they have died and this would have been considered completely impossible and miraculous even a 100 years ago.

In addition, if we are being scientifically honest, we should also say that the healing miracle stories are actually not that unusual. Since the spontaneous healing of any number of ailments is so common, it's not that far out of the realm of possibility that there was someone who was able to perform such healing on a fairly regular basis, a claim that isn't even unique to Jesus.

So far, these conclusions are relatively benign and boring; surely not worth the level of conflict that is often seen between 'science' and 'religion' in regard to Jesus! To say more, we need to look at the phenomenon of story creation and the relationship between experience, meaning, insight, and the mind.

If we examine our everyday experience, we know there are the basic facts of our experience and then the meaning of these facts. These two aspects of our lives are connected, but they are also different. One day at recess, two children play with a ball. For one child, this is the most exciting moment of her life and she goes on to become a professional athlete. For the other, it is one of many moments that are quickly forgotten. The material facts of the incidents are the same, the meaning is not. Furthermore, the meaning of an event may not be uncovered until long after the event and, in this example, the discovery of meaning can make the facts of the event, as we remember them, take on a miraculous quality.

We hear or see stories that contain deep meaning when people describe meeting a long lost love, or finding their true vocation after many years of unsatisfying work. They look back on their lives and remember the first moment when they thought of doing such work, or first met this person, and describe these times in a way that makes them glisten with a special magic.

Hearing this story, we can ask: Did that event *actually glisten with magic*? Another way of asking this question is to say: Is the meaning of that event real? In our time we are so attached to and distracted by the material world that we might answer the first question 'no' even as we would answer the second question 'yes'! In our mind we are thinking: "If I had a video tape of the moment he's describing I wouldn't see any magic" even while we know that the discovery of meaning in our lives is every bit as real and significant as the material facts of that same event.

Meaning in our lives is real because it's connected to that level of our being that makes us an alive human being. Meaning is connected to the image of God that I discussed in chapter 3. To describe the meaning of an event for a particular person is to describe how their mind interacts with their body and with creation to form them, and their lives, into something good and significant. This interaction of mind/body/spirit is magic! It's a unique moment in a unique life that can never be studied or repeated scientifically - even though this general pattern of how meaning is found and uncovered can be discussed.

The complex process that creates deep meaning renders the material facts of a particular event irrelevant in and of themselves. Facts only become significant when they take on meaning as these facts interact with the human mind. Furthermore, when these material facts take on significant meaning, they are transformed and a new layer of fact and value is added to them.

This process also works in reverse: from mind to matter. One truth about science that isn't well advertised is that many of the most important scientific discoveries aren't found through experimentation but are discovered in flashes of insight or dreams. A scientist wakes up in the morning and 'knows' the answer to the question she's been asking for years. Then when she goes into the lab, suddenly all of the data that she's been gathering looks different. The same computer printouts that didn't make sense before now fall into place and reveal a clear pattern. The mental insight, the discovery of meaning, has changed the material facts in front of her. Experimentation becomes the tool to confirm the insight, not discover it; once again mind and matter have interacted to reveal truth and create reality.

We're now in a position to say something more about Jesus and how he is also 'the Word made flesh.' For every gospel story, there are four people involved in relating to the tales of Jesus' life: Jesus, the disciples who told the stories, the followers who wrote the stories, and we who read the stories. For each of these people, mind and matter interact to help form and uncover meaning, material fact, and reality. From this perspective, we can ask not only what claims are being made about Jesus, but what do these claims mean and how can we understand them in a scientific age, even as we approach Jesus as someone unique?

The stories of Jesus tell of an encounter with someone who sees and experiences the world in a way that is different from us, even while sharing many of our same experiences. Even though the disciples, both ancient and modern, are often perplexed and confused by Jesus, they also see in him something wonderful and beautiful. A human being as human beings are supposed to be. This is what we find compelling about Jesus. It's not just material miracles that are significant. If he did these miracles and then was mean to people, we wouldn't care about the miracles. What is significant is the way that Jesus' mind interacts with the creation around him. It's what people hear and experience in conjunction with the material facts of Jesus that make him important.

What people saw in Jesus, and then tried to describe to others through their accounts, was the mind of the universe, the mind of creation, becoming present in a human form. When this occurred, amazing things happened. Without the fallen process of ego to obscure the process of Creation, Jesus is freed to live as the One who creates the Kingdom of God, the place where life, including fully formed human life, can live as the Good Creation. When Jesus describes being free from the powers of the world, this is what He means: a mind that is free of ego is also free of fear, and ultimately is free of death. He is the anointed One, the Christ, of God.

One hypothesis about spontaneous healing is that such healing occurs at a moment when our minds are open to healing. The physician who healed the boy with hypnosis did so before he knew that the boy's disease was incurable. Once he found that out, he couldn't repeat the miracle. What if the state of openness to the mind that is God became stable in a material person? This is what we who are followers of the one we call the Christ can claim in our modern era: Jesus was the One whose individual mind aligned fully, completely, and in a stable and consistent manner, with the mind of God, and as such was the mind of God.

In the subsequent Christian experience, when contemplatives have tried to describe the union with God, they describe intense experiences similar to the events in the gospels. Furthermore, those around these contemplatives describe experiences of healing, miraculous events such as flying, and other activities that mimic the Gospel miracle stories.

Returning to the categories of common but unique events that frustrate science, we see that these events are of the kind where mind and matter interact in a manner that is different from our normal experience. These occur when there are 'open moments,' times when our normal, fallen, ego patterns of mind stop, even if for an instant, and the mind of a creative and loving God can enter into our lives and do something amazing, or different. Mind and matter interact to form a transformed world. But then the moment passes and the world reverts to what we describe as 'normal.'

The reason that these phenomenon are so hard to study by our science is that our science is done by us; people with minds that are formed by ego and habit. When we go to experiment on matter to try and experience the 'non-fallen' world, the world as fully experienced by the mind of God, we cannot, by force of will, control the activity of the non-fallen experience.

In Jesus we experience a person whose mind isn't constantly formed by habit but rather is formed by God. So he is experienced in ways that are amazing and unique, and this experience is stable, not flickering as in our case.

Jesus, when seen and understood in this way, is revealed in a manner consistent with our current understanding of reality as well as with our Biblical and theological faith assertions. From an evolutionary perspective, the appearance of such a person within society is not inconsistent with what we understand about the development of species. Once humans with fully formed minds appeared on the scene, it is reasonable that at some point one of them would appear with a mind that not only had the capacity of awareness, but also had the capacity to remain aligned with the mind that initially created reality. This person we can claim as the Christ, even as we continue to wonder about and be amazed at what happened so many years ago.

However, this claim and the awe that it may inspire, isn't an end in and of itself. Jesus wasn't simply a curiosity or an isolated individual. Christianity describes both the person of Jesus and also the works of Jesus. As I mentioned at the beginning of the chapter, Christianity asserts that Jesus came here for some particular reasons. Having discussed the Creation, God, and humanity from a non-TSU perspective, I can now move to a discussion of theological categories related to the work of Jesus, those that deal with the relationship between God and humanity: salvation and judgement.

Chapter 6

Salvation

What is the point of religion? The answer may appear obvious, but it's something we need to remind ourselves of, particularly when we get too caught up in worrying about church budgets, committees, or some other aspect of the 'work' of the church. At its core, religion exists because human beings feel that we need help from somewhere and someone beyond ourselves. We recognize that we are a mess, we are *in* a mess, and we'd like to get out of the mess; but we know that we cannot do it alone: after all if we could, wouldn't we? Different faiths address the problems faced by humanity in slightly different ways, however the idea that there is a new approach needed to make life better is common to all religions.

In the Christian faith, this basic religious impulse has been called Salvation. If humanity is Fallen and is inexorably bound up with sin, then we need to be Saved; we need a way out. The Way was even the first name give to Christianity; people who followed Jesus were people of The Way, the way to being Saved. Once we understand the basic point of our faith, we can then ask what this salvation thing means: what are we being saved from and what are we being saved to? Christianity sees sin and the Fall as the problem, and it sees the solution as changing the results of the Fall. In traditional language we move from death into life. Jesus talked about inheriting the Kingdom of God: salvation is about changing our residence so to speak from the kingdom of the earth to the Kingdom of Heaven.

This Kingdom model of salvation is common throughout the Bible and usually describes the establishment of an earthly kingdom. In the Exodus story the people are freed from slavery and promised a land flowing with milk and honey. With the giving of the Law, Israel is told to follow the Law to create the good kingdom. This is a constant struggle and the kingdom veers off course, resulting in a bad kingdom that is often punished and even destroyed. Prophets arise to admonish and encourage the kingdom to return to the ways of God, usually with limited success.

Another model or image of salvation in the Bible is that of the refiners' fire. Just as ore is converted from an ugly rock into a beautiful metal through the process of smelting at high temperature, so too we are 'fired' in order to reveal the pure image of God that lies within us.

In Jesus' time, and then into the time of the earliest Church, the most common understanding of Christian salvation was the establishment of the Kingdom of God on earth with Jesus, or the returning Jesus, as king. However, as time went on and Jesus didn't come back, Salvation slowly began to be integrated into the TSU model of reality. Salvation, increasingly, became about what happened after you died. Like the image of God, Salvation was understood in spatial terms: if you were saved you were going up, if you weren't you were going down.

Tying Salvation to the TSU had several effects upon both Christianity and the believer. First, the results of our faith were primarily deferred until after death - the 'pie in the sky when you die' concept. Of course there were also behaviors common to a good Christian, but these were either done to help earn or insure one's salvation, or they were seen as peripheral activities or good secondary goals. The primary issue was where you went after you died.

The second result, and this has become more prominent in the scientific age, is that Salvation became nebulous because it is about times and places of which we have no direct experience. We can't see either heaven or hell and we can't talk to anyone who's been there, and so the whole faith endeavor has become increasingly vague[5]; which leads to the third major result of deferring salvation primarily until after death.

Once Salvation became about times and places of which we have no direct knowledge, the door was opened for religion to become about fear, power, and control. Ironically these are the very things that Jesus didn't want religion to be about. If Salvation is primarily concerned with which way the elevator goes after death, religious officials soon realized that they could terrify, and thus control, people by claiming that they had the power to determine the direction of the elevator based upon people's behavior, attitudes, and actions.

Once Christianity became the official religion of the Roman Empire, it became more tempting to use the faith in a controlling fashion. As a result generations have been raised to spend their lives afraid of what God will do to them after death. Children worry what will happen to them if they die before they get to confess their latest sin, adults are sick and anxious wondering if they are going to make it to heaven after death knowing how imperfect they are in life, family members grieve certain they will never see their non-believing relatives in Heaven.

This view of Salvation is problematic for another, more theological, reason; it doesn't solve the problem that

---

[5] We can see this problem playing itself out through the immense popularity of books about near death experiences. People of faith want to hear from people who have 'been' to heaven!

Salvation is supposed to address, sin on earth. If Salvation was originally defined as God helping humanity fix the problem of the Fall, then a Salvation that is primarily about what happens after death, doesn't solve this problem. The earth stays as fallen as ever while dead people are busy heading 'up' or 'down.' The Kingdom image is the most common Biblical image for Salvation because a change on earth from a bad kingdom run by human greed and ego to a good one ruled by God is a solution to the problem of a Fallen world.

These issues with the doctrine of Salvation have now become even more difficult as we have moved to an era that is dominated by a non-TSU view of reality. Not only are more people unwilling to be abused by religion, and this is a very good thing, but a salvation story that is based upon a spatial reality that we know doesn't exist, makes Christianity even less attractive to many (I will discuss Heaven and Hell as places more specifically in later chapters).

The response to this problem by different Christians and Christian churches has run the full spectrum from eliminating Salvation as an issue altogether, to holding on to the TSU view with great vigor. This spectrum, of course, corresponds to how these communities relate to science and how hostile they are to a scientific world view; the more hostile, the more the TSU view dominates the theology.

As with the previous topics, approaches that fail to directly integrate our knowledge of reality are unsatisfactory. On the one hand, a religion without Salvation is pointless; if we don't need any help, then why bother worrying about God. On the other, a Salvation narrative that not only isn't very in tune with the Bible - a non-earthly salvation - but also is out of touch with reality isn't valuable or helpful either. The silent, somewhat mushy middle ground (probably the most common stance) - mentioning Salvation but not having a clear sense of how it works or what it is - doesn't give our faith the robust, serious, qualities it deserves.

To understand Salvation in a non-TSU universe, we need to begin with the problem that Salvation purports to solve: sin. Sin can be understood in many different ways. Most commonly sin is seen as bad acts. There are lists of sins. Certain actions are 'good' and certain actions are 'bad.' The bad ones are sinful. Unfortunately this understanding of sin is both simplistic and problematic. Just as with the Salvation-after-death model, once sin is defined exclusively as 'bad acts' then the issue arises of who defines which acts are bad. Again, the problem of power over others in the religious sphere has led to massive amounts of abuse and control of people, particularly over women and religious and ethnic minority groups. But sin as bad behavior is also problematic theologically and practically.

Anyone who has even briefly thought about their actions knows that some behaviors are good in some circumstances and bad in others. Then there are the actions of groups of people - organizations, tribes, countries - which can be bad even as the individuals are perhaps trying to be good. It is challenging to understand this phenomenon within a simple model of sin as behavior. Finally, we know that refraining completely from bad actions is impossible even when we are trying hard to be good. These observations lead to the conclusion that sin is something deeper and more profound than just actions and behaviors in and of themselves; although certainly actions can be bad.

In the chapter on humanity, I discussed that sin had, at its root, the change in mind that accompanied the development of awareness, of a separate self. Before Adam and Eve were aware, they didn't see themselves as separate beings. Once they knew things, they had the ability to make judgements and to see themselves as separate from the rest of the world. This causes numerous problems for them and begins a chain of events leading to the first murder: Cain kills Abel because he is jealous and feels judged as inferior and distant from God, and human violence is unleashed upon the world.

Thus the problem of sin is a problem that has its root in the process of ego development. This is how we all share in the reality of sin; we all have minds that are capable of creating egos; and while an ego is necessary to function in the world, it is also the source of all our discord. What we need saving from is ourselves!

In Jesus we saw a mind synchronized with the mind of God, not just occasionally, or for a second, but permanently. His wasn't a separate ego, rather his mind was seamlessly one with God and this allowed him to be obedient unto death. When we say Jesus was without sin yet also human this is what we mean: he was aware, but not ego driven.

Salvation in the non-TSU world takes on a distinctly non-spatial character when sin and Jesus are understood in this new way. Such an image of salvation is more in line with the refining images of the Bible or the image of contemplative union given to us by the tradition of spiritual practice. It is also what Paul means as he calls us to take on the mind of Christ.

In our baptism liturgies we say that through baptism we are joined with Christ, the old is put aside and the new is put on. What we are joined to is the way of union with God, it is the path to being in our right mind, the mind that finds ourselves fully embracing the image of God given to us at our creation.

This understanding of Salvation is independent of bodily life or death and exists on a continuum of fulfillment. If we choose to fully embrace our spiritual lives while on earth, we can begin to experience the fruits of Salvation here and now. As Jesus would tell people when they had a moment of great realization: you are not far from the Kingdom of God. On the other hand, transformation beyond death isn't excluded from this view of Salvation. Any transformation we continue to experience after death is simply the culmination of our Salvation experience.

However, as Christians who follow the One who was concerned with the condition of people here on earth, as inhabitants of a creation that groans for something new, something better, we must realize that the main stage for the work of Salvation is here and now, not far away and later. This is a wonderful realization. Salvation is no longer a vague and mysterious condition whose rules are governed by those with ecclesial power. Rather it is a vibrant and important part of our everyday lives that we can embrace and journey towards using the tools of the spiritual life.

Given this vision of the nature of Salvation, we are now in a position to address a closely related doctrine, Judgement, as well as the means to Salvation, grace.

Chapter 7

Judgement and Grace

If Salvation is what happens when God's face shines favorably upon us, then judgement and grace are the means, or tools, that God uses in the process of saving humanity. It's not very often that grace and judgement are considered together in a positive light. My experience is that judgement is often portrayed as the negative thing that God does when we don't respond to the good gifts that God offers us through grace. However I would suggest that this is an incorrect view of judgement, and that grace and judgement work together and are two sides of the same coin: they are the currency of God's love for us. In this chapter I describe how judgement and grace work and how they can be understood outside of the TSU.

On a most basic level, grace can be understood as the ground, or fundamental stance of God in relation to humanity and the created world. God loves God's creation and desires nothing but the best for it. At the same time God makes judgements, assessments of our condition and actions, and responds to these appropriately and graciously. In the Bible judgement has a distinctly legal characteristic. People have sinned and fallen short in relation to the Law and God is the Judge who metes out punishments for the crimes committed by the nation, the people of God. Some of the results of God's judgement are exile, destruction of the Temple, and death.

However these negative results are never the last word. God is always working to redeem God's people, to restore them to goodness and righteousness. The impulse to heal and rebuild is the impulse of grace. God gathers the people like a mother hen; God brings them from afar and rebuilds the Holy City; God heals those who have been told they are unloveable; and restores the mind of the demoniac. These are the acts of a gracious God.

As Christianity developed, both judgement and grace continued to be important attributes of God; however judgement, harsh judgement, was often emphasized more than grace. Within the TSU, as salvation increasingly became about what occurred after death, judgement and grace also became connected to the spatial construction of the universe and was the process by which God decided who went up and who went down.

When this function was connected to the apocalyptic visions of books such as Daniel and the Revelation, judgement was cast in terrifying spatial terms and grace often disappeared altogether: God comes out of the sky with tremendous power and force, rending the heavens and causing havoc on earth. This vision of the end times and God's judgement is still popular in certain Christian circles, as interest in the Left Behind book series indicates. On a smaller scale, I've had many older church members tell me about the pastors of their youth who pounded the pulpit week after week talking about the terrifying power of God's judgement and the ability to send them to Hell. One woman recently told me how she would never have considered talking to her childhood pastor, "He was too scary." This, of course, was also her childhood image of God. Judgement reigned supreme and grace had vanished almost entirely.

Within other Christian circles, the Judgement of God is problematic and has even fallen out of favor. Part of this phenomenon has to do with the terror that accompanies some of the more traditional views of this doctrine. A monstrous figure appearing out of the sky to destroy civilization doesn't sit well with people who take seriously the notion that God is love. Problems with judgement also arise from its connection to the TSU model of reality. We know that there isn't a super-large creature sitting on a clear dome above us, looking down, judging our every move.

These challenges have led some to discard the notion of God's judgement, much like they have discarded the concept of sin. Their reasoning is that if God is infinitely loving, then somehow judgement isn't necessary. In churches with this approach one might expect to find a stronger notion of God's grace, however often this isn't true. Ironically when judgement disappears, grace becomes watered down and intangible, undefined, and simply some vague and general notion that 'God is good.'

Both of these approaches, the traditional terrifying judge and the nonexistent judge, are highly problematic. The former doesn't work because the huge monster image certainly doesn't fit with the images of Jesus we have in the gospels. If we are serious about our assertion that in Jesus we see God, then it's difficult to square Him with the big cosmic torturer. The spatial problems created by the TSU add further challenges to this image of judgement.

However, discarding judgement doesn't work either because our faith has a strong commitment to justice. We know that the world is a very broken, disturbed and disturbing place. Every day people are tortured, starved, oppressed, killed, and sold into slavery. Don't we 'judge' these things as wrong? Don't we want the world, the universe, to be a better place? Of course we do, and not only do we want a transformed, good, Creation, but we claim that God is working towards a just, good, peaceful state of affairs. Therefore, we cannot simply do away with the theological notion of judgement, any more than we can do away with the reality of God.

In addition, neither of these positions suit grace very well either. The first makes grace non-existent. The second turns grace into an 'I'm ok, you're ok' pop-psychology. In a scientific world, it cannot be imagined how either judgement or grace can function well. Yet if God exists and is real, then the judgement and grace of God, the actions of God that works towards, insists on, good must also be real. What we need is an imaginative understanding of God's judgement and grace that remains true to our faith and makes sense in our current reality.

Any modern discussion of judgement and grace begins with the nature and structure of the universe as we find it. Science has been marvelously successful at describing and discovering what we now refer to as the 'laws of nature;' sets of rules that govern the material universe. Yet the popular understanding of this term, laws of nature, is a bit misleading. Scientific discovery is always giving us new and nuanced views of material reality, and what was a law today can be a discarded concept a decade from now. However, on the level of large structures, the macroscopic level, many of the laws of motion, for example, are still excellent approximations of the reality we experience every day.

Beyond the specifics of any given law, is the fundamental discovery and understanding that there are laws at all. The universe can be described by concepts that we discover! If the universe had no laws, we would have no idea what was going on from moment to moment, if we could even exist at all which, without such regularity, we probably couldn't. If we examine the concept of scientific 'law' itself (and it is interesting that we even use this word for our concepts about nature, because it implies a legal, or regulated, system) we can see embedded within every law the reality of cause and effect. If I'm standing on a planet and I drop a ball, it will fall to the planet's surface in a way that I can calculate. If I am the particular life form we call an animal I will have certain kinds of cells and those cells will function in certain ways as determined by the contents of the cell, most particularly by the contents of the DNA of that cell. If I jump off a very high cliff I will hurt myself because I will fall to the ground below.

Parents work hard to teach their children about the cause and effect reality of our world. We spend thousands of hours telling our kids not to touch hot things, not to put their toys in electrical outlets, not to put tiny objects up their nose, and to look both ways when they cross the street. We perform this educational task because we know that the world does have this quality of law and predictability. We also perform this task because we love our kids and we want them to be able to function well in the world. If you sometimes won the lottery by putting a dry bean in your ear, then you wouldn't warn your children against such an activity. If things were completely random an education about cause and effect would be a waste of time.

Many who have adopted an anti-faith stance in the modern era, have used the existence of such laws as an argument against faith. They reason that if the universe is governed by predictable laws, and such laws describe the cause and effect reality we live in, then there is no need to invoke a God as an actor in the world. However, the writers of the Bible knew about the reality of cause and effect in the world, but rather than using this fact to dismiss God, they used it as a sign of God's existence and also employed the term law to describe the way that God orders reality. The book of Proverbs is a meditation on the cause and effect nature of our lives: if you follow the laws of God, good things happen, if not, bad things happen.

As theological judgement became more about final judgement after death, and less about present judgement in life, and grace became more about whether you lucked out enough to go to heaven when you died, we lost the understanding that judgement and grace are enshrined in the very nature of reality.

A cause and effect world is a world of both judgement and grace. One of the manifestations of sin is our desire to deny this truth and to try and escape the consequences of our actions. In the modern era, global warming is an excellent example of this denial. Humanity wants to try and pretend that we can pump as much carbon dioxide into the atmosphere as we want without consequence. This is simply not true, as we can see by examining Venus. If we continue to pollute the atmosphere with such greenhouse gases we will be 'judged' on our actions with the resulting warming of the earth and the negative effects that follow. Simultaneously, the fact that we can understand how our actions effect our environment on both a large and small level, is indicative of the ever present reality of grace.

Thus one way of understanding judgement and grace in our modern era is to embrace, once again, the ancient view that these are qualities of God embedded in a cause and effect world. Divine judgement is simply the consequences of our actions. Grace is the reality that God is always working for the best in every situation, helping to bring good into and out of any situation. Science has confirmed for us the truth that we live in a lawful world. This is a gracious work of God, not a consequence of chance or random event. Bringing judgement into the present is invigorating and powerful because it shows us how much responsibility God has in fact given us. Through our actions we have the power to shape reality in this lawful universe.

Of course this is only part of the story. Biblical wisdom literature also reflects the knowledge that 'bad things happen to good people.' The book of Job is a meditation on this truth. The Bible observes on several occasions that the wicked prosper and the good go down into the dust. In our own times we are very aware of this truth. How do these realities fit into God's judgement and God's grace?

In part, it was this observation about the seemingly unjust nature of human society and the world that led to judgement being pushed back until after death. If God's judgement doesn't appear to work too well on earth, it must work perfectly in Heaven. Such logic also fuels the apocalyptic vision. If people don't take the subtle, or not so subtle, hints that God gives us, like exile or the destruction of the temple, then God will appear out of the clouds and clobber us: surely that will get our attention. Perhaps it's the only solution to the unjust mess on earth. How do we address these questions in a modern world?

The observation that judgement and grace are built into the cause and effect nature of reality is an observation about what is called 'bottom-up' causality. This means that actions, laws, and events on the smallest levels of the world influence what happens on larger levels of reality. An example of this is our genetics. The order and configuration of our DNA, very tiny molecules, influences and causes things that we see on the macroscopic level, our eye color, our sex, even parts of our personality. So God's judgement acts in this bottom-up manner because all of reality is at least somewhat constrained by laws that result in consequences from actions.

However there is also such a thing as top-down causation. This is where events at a higher level of order or reality influence or create effects at lower levels of reality. One example of this would be that our decision to spend too much time in the sun can cause damage to our DNA which can result in skin cancer. Our mental decision resulted in biochemical effects that resulted in an illness caused by the changes on the molecular level.

The images of judgement after death, or God coming out of the sky, are descriptions of top-down causation. These are theological statements that affirm that God is at the 'top' of all causes and that sooner or later God will prevail.

In previous chapters I discussed how sin is a manifestation of a mind that is disconnected from the mind of God. We can certainly imagine that in a world of billions of such minds, there are numerous actions that can result in the good perishing and the evil prospering. In our created state, our minds are allowed to function as if they are independent entities; God has given us the space to be self-aware and yet also self-centered.

Because mind can exert top-down causation on the world, our minds can create scenarios where the bottom-up cause and effect judgement is held at bay, at least for a while. Again, global warming is a good example. We have been able to 'get away with' polluting the atmosphere for a long time because earth is quite large and it is a very complex system with many healing control mechanisms that have kept the climate within a certain range that is hospitable for life. However, at a certain point, the bottom up causes and the top down causes clash and we can no longer avoid the consequences of our actions.

God's judgement and grace can be understood as exerting both bottom up and top down effects. In the previous chapter Salvation was understood as the purification process by which the image of God within each person is revealed. Ultimately, perhaps after death, but perhaps before, God's mind reaches into ours and purges it of all that is dross and evil. This action of God's mind upon and within our mind to purify and transform is the action of grace.

From this perspective the process of grace and judgement - God's mind acting within and through our minds - is a top down cause that ultimately results in us becoming the people God wants us to be. We have all heard stories of people having great realizations about themselves and the evil they are doing, flashes of insight that change them forever. The hymn Amazing Grace resulted from one such moment of change; a slave trader realized the errors of his ways and became a strong voice for abolition. This was a moment of God's judgement reaching into this man's mind and changing him for the good; an act he recognized as gracious. The bottom up causes of the evil he was involved with hadn't penetrated through to his consciousness and so God used the top down method.

We can see this manifestation of God's grace work in meditation retreats. I've run and participated in dozens of such retreats over the years and my colleagues and I have often noted how 'God always shows up' in such events. If God's grace wasn't a permanent fixture in the working of the universe then this wouldn't be the case. People would go on retreat and 'nothing would happen.' Yet I have never known this to be the case. Rather the grace of God is a powerful and constant mental presence in the world that anyone can connect with at any time. This is why grace is so special and why Christianity claims that it isn't earned but rather is given through faith. It's always there, always available, and always ready to become a force for good in our lives.

Scientists often talk about the 'boundary conditions' for certain phenomenon. For example the speed of light is a famous boundary condition; nothing can, at least as far as we know, accelerate past the speed of light. The image of judgement and grace that I have offered here is that they are a boundary condition for our existence. We are bounded both from below and from above by the reality of God's law. From below, God's grace and judgement weaves cause and effect into the very fabric of reality and rewards our actions with consequences and with a movement towards the good. From above, God's judgement and grace exerts final causation on all of creation because the mind of God has the final say over the course of our lives and the life of the universe.

As with salvation, judgement and grace can be understood in the modern world by uncoupling the theological description from a spatial configuration of the TSU. However, now that we have moved so much out of the ancient spaces of our faith, what do we do with Heaven and Hell, the top and bottom story of the ancient Christian universe? This is the question I take up in the next two chapters.

Chapter 8

Heaven

For many, perhaps most, Christians getting to Heaven is the number one goal of their faith. Images of a positive eternity have encouraged people for generations. This, coupled with the desires to avoid Hell, and to see relatives and friends who have died, have provided strong motivation to believers. These classical images of Heaven are drawn from the TSU model of reality. Heaven is a good place "up there," Heaven is full of heavenly beings floating around on clouds, and of course, God, an old man, sits on a throne in the middle of it all. Into the present day our culture is full of references, jokes, songs, and stories that are grounded in this view of reality. Recently a friend visited a brand new modern church where the wall at the front of the sanctuary was painted with a picture of angels and Jesus sitting on the clouds.

Because the motivation to get to Heaven, and the claim that such a place is real, is so powerful, people hold onto these images even as their literal truth have been understood to be false for many years. As with the entire TSU model of reality, the ancient view of Heaven remains because there is no alternative; and to even discuss an alternative is taken to mean that one is getting rid of Heaven entirely. Recently, a church member accused me of doing just that, and was livid because "if Heaven isn't real then there isn't any point in my being good now."

In previous chapters I have focused on removing the spatial orientation of various doctrines and theological concepts in order to bring them into the modern era. This conceptual move is necessary because the TSU is no longer a valid view of reality. Yet removing these spatial considerations threatens the notion, or validity, of theological concepts that aren't part of the material universe as we currently understand it. So does Heaven disappear in a non-TSU model of reality? No. However as before, we must reconfigure our understanding of Heaven so that we can make sense of it today. To accomplish this task I will begin with Biblical reflections upon Heaven, and then proceed to a discussion of consciousness in the material world.

Although the Heavenly realms are present throughout the Bible, it is only in the New Testament that the concept of people being in Heaven, or in the Kingdom of Heaven, begins to emerge as a strong theme. In the Old Testament, the Heavenly realms are the home of God and the Heavenly beings. The spatial reality that is connected to salvation occurs here on earth and is related to the establishment of the righteous kingdom of Israel where the good king will rule according to God's law. Many of Jesus' disciples thought he was going to become King in Jerusalem because they had been raised to understand that the earth was the place of salvation. Even in the apocalyptic vision of Daniel, God comes out of the sky to establish His good kingdom on earth. So Heaven wasn't a place where people 'went.'

In the New Testament this situation begins to change somewhat, although not nearly as much as later Christians have come to believe. Jesus spent much of his time talking about the Kingdom of God, or the Kingdom of Heaven. From the perspective of Christianity as it developed, these terms became synonymous with the Heaven that we now think about: the place in the sky. However Jesus' comments about these Kingdoms are not so clearly directed to a space above the earth. Sometimes he claims that people are near to the Kingdom right now. Sometimes he says that the Kingdom is within you. Sometimes he indicates that the Kingdom appears when good deeds are done. Then, on a few occasions, the Kingdom is associated with an afterlife experience.

Jesus, through his teachings, explicitly develops the understanding that one of the goals of our faith is to enter the Kingdom of God. Although firmly grounded in the classic Hebrew vision of the good Kingdom, Jesus lays the groundwork for our understanding that God is trying to help us 'get to' Heaven. As Christianity developed, and Jesus didn't return to establish a kingdom on earth, this idea of getting to Heaven became more prominent in Christian theology. This in turn solidified Heaven as a physical place where we would 'go,' and such a place was available through the model of the TSU.

But if we look carefully at the full range of Jesus' examples about the Kingdom of God we see that He wasn't talking so much about a physical place, but rather a changed state of being. The Kingdom of God was said to be near or could be entered when someone truly understood the Law, or when people appeared in a community to heal and teach, or when someone cared for the least of these. Furthermore Jesus specifically said that the Kingdom was within us and not some place outside of us. Keeping in mind this important set of observations, we can turn to a discussion of consciousness and physicality, specifically consciousness and three dimensional space.

We live in what we call three dimensional space. Adding time to our consideration gives us what has been called four dimensional space-time. Within this dimensional reality we live our lives, have our relationships, experience everything that we know and love. As I discussed in previous chapters our very Selves are formed by the experience of space-time as chronicled by our senses. Thus when we consider an eternal life, it is natural for us to think of this life as occurring in a condition similar to what we know now. This is the reason that Heaven as a 'place' is so appealing; we know what places are like.

However we also have the experience of our minds, and this process of our mind is both connected to our physicality and is independent of our physical state. For example, we talk about 'going somewhere in our imagination.' This expression describes the experience of sitting in one place while we think about all manner of other places or experiences. Powerful memories are said to 'bring us back' to a particular place and time. Dreams are yet another example of an experience that appears separate from physical space and time. Now in our modern world, we even have 'virtual reality,' the electronic space where we spend more and more time each day.

When faced with non-material experience our tendency, arising from the training we've gotten living within a physical space, is to say that these flights of mind are *not as real* as our experience within the physical world. We even have expressions like 'it's all in your head' or 'you're just imagining things' to reinforce this hierarchy of what is real and what is not. Yet the interest, even the obsession, that we now have with the internet shows that we are convinced that a reality constructed out of the movement of electrons through various devices is quite real and important.

The essential question in this debate is whether or not consciousness is 'real' and whether or not it can exist separately from our physical brains. Throughout this book I have made both the assumption and the assertion that it can:

mind doesn't require a physical brain to exist. Contemplatives have maintained this position for thousands of years; yet until recently much of science has rejected it with great vigor. However, there is a growing body of evidence coming from the scientific community that supports the notion that consciousness can exist separately from our bodies.[6]

We are also aware of the effect that our state of mind can have upon our perception of reality. We start the day feeling great and happy and thinking that the world is wonderful, only to be derailed by an incident that suddenly makes us feel horrible. Now our lives are a mess and we are upset and the world is hostile and unfriendly. What has changed in this sequence of events is our minds and the effect that our mind has upon our experience of the world.

These observations emphasize that reality includes more than just our four dimensional space-time. The world of our mind is real and substantial and has a life of its own that shouldn't be dismissed as 'our imagination.' Furthermore when discussing something like Heaven, we shouldn't try to form our conceptions of heaven around a physical space just because we are used to considering physical spaces to be the only 'real' spaces.

Returning to the words of Jesus, his comments about the Kingdom of God are congruent with these modern observations about mind and reality. Taking his examples as a whole, we can see that Jesus was describing God's

---

[6] Some of the areas of study looking into this issue are the studies of Near Death Experiences, Energy Medicine, Artificial Intelligence, and certain aspects of neuropsychology. Within the scientific community there is still tremendous debate, discussion, and dissension regarding this topic.

Kingdom as a fluid, present, yet also future entity whose presence in our lives depends more upon our state of being then upon where we are physically located.

In a non-TSU reality, Heaven is a real place that doesn't necessarily have a three dimensional space associated with it. In our current physical lives, Heaven can indeed pass near to us when we are one with the mind of Christ. After we die, and our consciousness is purified according to God's judgement and grace, the Heavenly realm is open to our consciousness, although we certainly don't understand the exact nature of that experience. Perhaps it is more like our dream states, fluid, spacious and amazing. Perhaps it is like floating in the air such that we can choose to go anywhere in the universe. Perhaps it is like nothing we can even imagine.

One of the most interesting discoveries of modern physics is the presence of 'dark' matter and energy in the universe. What this 'stuff' is we don't yet understand with great precision, but it's scientifically accepted that there exists a vast amount of material that is part of the universe and is unaffected by visible light. Not only can we not see dark matter or energy, but the amount of material that is 'out there' dwarfs what we can see. Current estimates are that the universe is composed of about 95% dark material! What would happen if consciousness could attach to dark matter in the same way that it has attached to light matter through our brains? It's perfectly reasonable to assume that this is possible. Maybe the Heavenly realms are the realms of dark matter and energy and when we 'go to' Heaven our consciousness transitions over from light to dark matter. Of course such material is only dark and light relative to us! When we are conscious within what we now call dark matter, we may find that it is very light indeed.

Whatever the specifics, Heaven is a place of consciousness both for here and now as well as then and beyond.

Chapter 9

Hell

The TSU has always had a basement, the lower story. In this chapter I will explore the nature of this lower story, what Christianity came to call Hell, the problems with our traditional view of Hell, and then move on to a modern vision of this theological principle.

In the Old Testament, the lower story was called Sheol and it was not the same as what we now call Hell. Rather it was a dull, nondescript place where *everyone* went after they died to await a final restoration of the earth. By the time of Jesus, the entire Mediterranean world had been influenced by Greek thought, and Hades was a familiar concept for the underworld, although Hades didn't really fit theologically into traditional Jewish thought. Thus in the gospels there are actually two completely different terms used by Jesus, both of which are commonly translated into English as "Hell."

The first term is Hades, the Greek land of the shades. Since this was a term from Greek religion, its meaning to first century Jews is somewhat vague. To some it was probably just the Greek word for Sheol. To others, who were more influenced by Greek thought and culture, it was perhaps seen as a place of torment, a place you wouldn't want to go.

The second term is Gehenna. This was the garbage dump on the outskirts of Jerusalem where city refuse and anything that was considered impure and unclean was taken to be burned. I imagine it was a very unpleasant place, and it was a place that was ritually unclean. Thus anything that went there was considered to be outside the realm of God.

Because burning things to remove waste and dross was both a common Biblical image and a practical experience it was possible, as Christianity grew, to consolidate these Biblical references and terms - fire, Hades, Gehenna - into the Christian concept of Hell: a horrible underworld separate from God and a place of pain, burning, and torture. Once developed, the primary purpose of such a theological concept was to scare and control people into doing 'good,' or whatever the church said was good, now on earth.

This purpose alone is enough to make the entire Hell project suspect, especially as the fully formed concept isn't Scriptural. As the idea grew and became more important in Christianity, Hell had nothing to do with cosmology, either ancient or modern, but rather had to do with the psychology of faith and issues of authority, domination, and motivation for belief. Thus in order to say something about how Hell might be integrated into a non-TSU view of reality, we need to look closely at what Hell, the concept, is trying to say theologically and also what it describes practically.

Theologically, the idea of Hell is attached to Judgement. People supposedly end up in Hell because they are Judged and found unworthy of participating in eternal life with God. In this view, Hell exists because God needs some place to put all the people who are bad, in some way or another, and keep them away from all the good people who are having fun in Heaven. What constitutes 'bad' varies depending on which particular brand of Christianity one is talking about.

For some, bad consists of violating 'the rules,' as determined by the church; at times bad has simply meant dying without confessing and repenting of sin; bad can also mean not accepting Jesus as your Savior, and for some this category includes people who haven't even ever heard of Jesus! This is a wide range of reasons for going to Hell; and some of them, particularly that of people who haven't even heard of Jesus, make it quite difficult to see how the reason invoked can be connected to God's Judgement in any good or rational way.

In our current setting, Judgement and Hell are connected in a manner that creates discomfort with both concepts. There are three problems: the first arises from the nature of God, the second from the nature of justice, the third from the nature of people.

First, it's hard to equate an eternal torture chamber with a loving God. There is simply no rational, true definition of love that fits with a desire to endlessly inflict pain. If God is fundamentally loving, then there is no way that God would sanction the creation of such a place. There have been many convoluted arguments used to try and get around this problem, but I would suggest that none of them is satisfactory.

The second concern relates to the nature of justice. We generally understand that true justice demands that 'the punishment fit the crime.' This view of justice is actually Biblical. God metes out punishment in proportion to the violation of the law. The Bible also emphasizes that God's punishment is tempered by God's mercy and desire to forgive. We recognize this through our own impulses to mete out punishment that is proportional to the crime. When children are 'naughty' we understand that you should punish them in a way that helps them become good. We even call parents whose punishments are too severe abusive. Given this understanding of justice it is very hard, I would suggest impossible, to imagine what crime people might commit that would deserve unending torture. This vision simply cannot be congruent with what we say of either God or justice.

The final objection to the vision of Hell as connected to Judgement has to do with what we know and say about people. If one of the purposes of Hell is to separate out good and bad people then we must think about people and whether this notion makes any sense. This idea of separation contradicts what we say theologically about people, not to mention what we all *know* about people, that we are all sinners and have all fallen short of the glory of God. If we are indeed all sinners then there aren't any purely good people who should go up and purely bad people who should go down.

This particular logic has been addressed by saying that Hell is for those who have intentionally resisted God and thus the judgement isn't about good or bad per se but rather about will and the awareness of one's badness and the desire to be good. But even this logic fails the test of our theological and common sense understanding. We all know that our will and our awareness change over time and aren't consistently good or bad; and this particular argument doesn't address all of the other reasons that have been given for sending people to Hell.

The other challenge to this, or any other argument for the existence of a traditional Hell, is the power of God. Christians claim that through the death and resurrection of Jesus, God has triumphed over sin, death, and Satan. We make a strong claim that God is more powerful than evil.

Generally we associate power with successful action. If a person is always failing at their endeavors we say that they don't have much power in the world, either economic power, or interpersonal power, or creative power, etc. If the traditional view of Hell is correct, then God fails to recover and redeem far more people than God saves. Hell is overpopulated and Heaven has plenty of wide open spaces. Certainly this arrangement appeals to people who consider themselves righteous, but from the point of view of creation, and all of humanity, such a result makes God look like a dismal failure, and this contradicts our claims about the work of Christ.

If going to Hell is an issue of will or intention, as some say, isn't God able to persuade us to engage God, either here when we are alive, or later after death?   It's highly inconsistent to say that God has tremendous power in the universe while at the same time declaring that God is almost a complete failure when it comes to the one area of theological work in which God intervened most directly.

These arguments make the connection of Judgement to the traditional view of Hell highly problematic indeed. Judgement as purification is a much more positive view that is consistent with all that we know of justice and the human person.   What we need, to be re-created as good, is a purification that reveals the person God wants us to be, not to be tortured for eternity.

The spatial issues with Hell in the TSU are equally problematic. As with the TSU version of Heaven, Hell as a lower story of material reality obviously doesn't exist.   In order to come up with a modern view of Hell that was consistent with science, we would have to imagine that God had somehow 'roped off' a part of the universe where all of these people were stashed forever, separate from everyone and every place else.   Although we might say that this is theoretically possible - maybe everyone ends up on a very hot planet or in the center of some star - it actually contradicts several fundamental principles of the universe.

The first is that our knowledge of the universe increasingly points towards an appreciation for the wholeness, or interconnectedness of material reality. All matter and energy come from the same place and have been 'entangled' since the beginning of Creation. This means that any true separation is impossible. We might like the idea of certain people being stashed away somewhere forever, but this idea isn't tenable with what we know of the creation in which we find ourselves.

The second problem is similar to the first but occurs on the level of mind. If indeed the afterlife realms consist of a new mental alignment with the material universe, then this state must be very fluid and far reaching in space and time. Furthermore, it connects to the wholeness that is the mind of God. To create some space fundamentally separate from this reality is logically inconsistent.

Given all of these objections and problem, both theological and material, why has the traditional view of Hell had such staying power? One reason is the fear factor that I've already mentioned. But there is another, I think, more powerful reason. Hell describes a place, a real physical place, where God is absent, that is a place of endless suffering. There is no way out, and as seen from inside such a place, there is also no obvious relief.

If we consider such a description, I would suggest that this describes one of the common human experiences of earth. With the exception of a very few people, most of humanity have experienced lives of great suffering and a lived experience of God being invisible and far away. War, famine, disease, and death have been the staples of daily existence, and this reality stretches endlessly from the present into both the past and the future, with, frankly, no end in sight.

The fact that humanity has been able to continue on and even find hope and joy in the midst of this suffering is a wonderful tribute to the Spirit of Life in our lives, but we cannot deny the truth of our experience of endless suffering. In some sense we might even compare our experience of Jesus here on earth to the claim that he descended to Sheol after his death.

The Church tradition teaches that Jesus descended to the lower story of the TSU to preach to the dead, the shades of the good news. How different is this from him coming down to earth to preach to us? Hell as a theological concept has been successful because humans have no trouble imagining it; even the church created torture chambers, so why not God? This projection onto eternity of the fallen and failed nature of humanity is a painful testimony to the power of our mental projections, and is also an important fact when we go to consider what a modern theological understanding of Hell might look like.

One approach to the modern vision is to simply eliminate Hell altogether from Christian theology. Many people have done this and I admit it's tempting. Tradition is the most significant problem with this approach. When conversing with our fellow people of faith, or even when talking with non-Christians, everyone knows that Hell has been, and in most circles still is, a part of Christian history and theology. Even if we don't like the idea, people are always very suspicious of an individual wiping away 2000 years of history just because they feel badly about that history. Even if we want to say that the concept has been a mistake, which I certainly do, I think it's more valuable to enter into the conversation about a concept and reformulate it in a way that makes sense (even if part of that reformulation is a dismissal of the past).

As with Heaven, we begin by asserting that a non-TSU understanding of Hell cannot be primarily spatial. The bottom story of the TSU doesn't exist as such. Thus a new vision of Hell arises from our new vision of Judgement, as well as from our understanding that Heaven and Hell as concepts primarily address the question of a mind that is, or is not, aligned with God.

Associating Heaven with a state of mind, or being, allowed for the possibility of transcending the dividing line of death. Heaven became accessible both now and later depending on one's state of mind. A modern view of Hell should embrace a similar perspective. If Hell is the condition that arises when one is intentionally, willfully, rejecting God, or when one is even not paying particular attention to God, then we can see that by our manner of life on earth, we choose to live in Hell. Our refusal to renounce war, violence, hatred, oppression, fear, and all manner of evil results in a state of unending suffering, far from God, for all of humanity. This is indeed Hell and it arises directly from the Judgement of God that is embedded in the reality of a causal world.

When we transition to the afterlife, we enter into the Judgement of God that is the causality from above, God's active purification of our mental habits and patterns. Although anything that can be said about this is speculative, it is interesting to imagine what such an activity might be like. Any purification would need to meet the demands of both justice and compassion. Perhaps we might experience all of the unresolved suffering that we had caused during our lifetime. Perhaps we simply need to see ourselves very clearly.

In contemplative practice, a situation where we are forced by the constraints of the practice to see our minds with increasing clarity, compassion arises as we are exposed to the truth of ourselves, our actions, and the harm that we have caused. This can be a very painful experience. Our ego, the habits and patterns of mind that keep us from seeing God's reality as it is, resists this examination and actively fights to maintain itself and our self-centered view of the world. Often times sessions of deep prayer are somewhat hellish. An extended purification process could certainly seem like Hell as we need to be melted down and refined into the pure image of God that has been gathering so much dross over the years.

In the afterlife then, Hell is the experience of our ego as it dissolves. Of course this is not torture on God's part, nor is it an eternal separation from God. Rather it is a glorious transformation that perhaps we only appreciate as such when we are finally out the other side.

The modern view of Hell is thus, as it should be, the mirror image of the view of Heaven. As we understand these concepts anew we have arrived at the complete collapse of the Three Story Universe. Hell is indeed that mental state in which we are far from God. This is a state that cuts across the transitional divide of death but, in a reversal from Heaven, Hell is more prominent on this side of death then on the farther shore. Hell is most obvious in this world, where we have the maximum space to exercise our own will. When we reach the realm where God is more directly involved, that place of Heavenly purification, Hell is not a place but the ego's experience of transformation; an experience whose intensity and duration may have a lot to do with how we have lived our lives, a topic I will address in greater detail in the last chapter.

Chapter 10

Scripture

Although I've referred to the Christian scripture, the Bible, throughout the preceding chapters, I have waited until the later part of the book to address the Bible directly. Scripture arises within the context of our material world and is written by people who live in that world, in a particular place and time. Therefore, it was important to address those realities - people and the created world - before the Bible, so that a non-TSU view of the Bible could be discussed. Furthermore, since the Bible is the source of the TSU vision of the universe, Scripture, and the theology that flows from it, presents a particular challenge to anyone who wishes to integrate the scientific view of reality with our faith.

What we now call the Bible was written over a period of approximately 750-1000 years in a time when human technology and material knowledge was vastly different than today. In addition, over 95% of the population was illiterate, and they learned about the world, God, and themselves, through spoken story. For most, life was short, harsh, highly unpredictable and unintelligible. Individual human beings were weak and expendable and the stage upon which they lived was small and immanent. By contrast the earth and cosmos seemed both powerful and mysterious. Finally, there was no reason to believe that earth was a tiny speck in an infinite expanse of space. Although such an environment was vastly different from our modern technological world, it was not so different from what most of humanity continued to experience until very recently.

Given what people knew and saw on a day to day basis, it isn't surprising that the TSU model of the universe came into being and was recorded in Scripture. It also isn't surprising that as conditions, technologies, and knowledge changed and departed from the Biblical reality, Scripture became the focal point of so much of the difficulty between science and faith.

Simply stated, the problem is this: if Scripture has authority as the 'true word of God,' as a unique revelation that tells us something about who and what God is and what God is up to in the world, how can it also contain a vision of reality that is, on the face of it, wrong?

For some, perhaps for an increasing number of people, this is not a problem. There are many who can understand the Bible such that the TSU content isn't problematic. One reason for this lack of concern is that there are fewer and fewer Christians who read the Bible or actually know anything of its content! I would venture to say that there's a direct correlation between those who don't read the Bible and those who aren't bothered by the TSU. When such people actually begin to read the Bible, they are often overwhelmed by how odd it is; how violent the stories are, how strange the images are, how foreign it seems. If our faith story simply consists of something like, "Jesus loves me this I know," then the rest of the Biblical content is irrelevant and the TSU vision of reality isn't too much of a problem; that is until someone who is a non-Christian asks us about it. At this point, one response is to simply discard or ignore large chunks of the Bible as being too primitive or out of touch with reality.

On the other hand, for those who are members of churches where the Bible is taken a bit more seriously, the presence of all of these strange stories and images is more challenging and needs to be addressed. These churches approach Scripture in numerous ways and run the theological gambit from 'liberal' to 'conservative'. Included in this group are those who are far more likely to be anti-science and to embrace certain views of reality that try to preserve some parts or aspects of a TSU cosmology. This would include Biblical literalists, young earth creationists, anti-evolutionists, or some variation of these positions and themes. Within churches that espouse these views, the Bible is embraced but often in a way that seems, from the point of view of science, ridiculous or at least very irrational and anti-intellectual.

I don't see either of these options, discarding large chunks of Scripture, or taking the Bible 'literally,' as being helpful to Christians in the 21st century. The former dilutes our faith and the authority of our Biblical text, and the later makes us sound like fools and is the source of much of the anti-Christian rhetoric that we hear today.

The alternative is to begin a modern discussion of the Bible and the TSU by answering the question: What kind of book is the Bible? In academic circles the question would be: What genre is the Bible? This isn't a question that most people consider, yet it's a question we all answer, even unconsciously when we pick up different books to read. We know that there are novels and text books and poetry books, as well as many other types of books, and when we read these different books we know instinctively what to expect and how to read each type of book. We wouldn't use a novel about outer space to teach us how to cook our steak, rather we would seek out a cookbook.

Over the past decade or so, we have become obsessed with 'true stories.' Movies make more money if the opening credits begin with the words "based on a true story;" reality TV is all the rage; and authors take great risks writing novels that are labeled memoirs so that they will sell more copies. We feel that if something is 'true' it is of great value and we also have a sense that if something is true we can capture it on video because it actually happened in the material world. Furthermore, science puts a very high value on truth claims, and it also defines truth, generally, as something that can be verified in the material plane of existence.

These views of truth and reality are what get us into trouble when we come to reading and evaluating the Bible. Because when we ask what kind of book the Bible is, we unconsciously feel that our only choices of categories are books that are 'true' and books that are 'fiction.' If we say the Bible isn't 'true' then we feel that we've undermined its authority as the word of God, and if we say it is 'true,' well then it must be in the same category of books as science text books and then we have to take the TSU, and all sorts of other things, much more literally. However there is another alternative.

The solution to this dilemma of truth vs fiction is to recognize that the Bible is another type of book altogether. Our Scripture is a book of sacred text, or spiritual teaching. We in the Christian west aren't generally familiar with this genre because most of us only read one such book, the Bible, and so we don't understand that our Scripture is a type of book of which there are many examples throughout history and even into the present day.

A sacred text is a book that attempts to speak the truth about the spiritual realities of the universe using many different forms of writing. Thus we realize that the Bible contains poetry, story, history, proverbs and other forms of literature, and all of these taken together are part of a book that seeks to speak the truth about God. Therefore, the truth that sacred texts reveal are truths about something larger than what is described in the book itself. The truth of sacred texts is revealed in a manner different from how a science text book describes what is true.

For example, when a biology book talks about a cell, and gives pictures and descriptions of a cell, it means to describe and depict something whose form and function is identical to what is shown in the book. On the other hand, when the Bible describes God as being like a mother hen who gathers her chicks together, we are not given to understand that there is a big chicken somewhere out in the universe and that's what God looks like! In our society, where science is king and we are obsessed with a certain kind of material truth, this understanding of the Bible as a Spiritual text is hard to grasp. We want to imagine that the stories in the Bible are something like a reality TV show and if David had a video camera, we could see Goliath getting hit with a stone on a You Tube video.

However, sacred texts don't operate in this manner, and frankly aren't even too concerned about such a definition of reality. Rather they tell the story of David and Goliath to teach us something about God; that God often raises up the weak and appears in unexpected places through unexpected people. This doesn't mean that *something* didn't happen that may have been like the story of David and Goliath, but rather that the material truth of the story shouldn't be our sole focus and concern as we read the text.

If we see the Bible as a spiritual text, then a non-TSU understanding and approach to scripture is not only possible, but it allows us to embrace all of the Bible and fully reclaim it as an authoritative revelation in the modern world.

Seen as sacred text, we realize that the entire Bible is the legacy of people who were trying to transmit truths about God using the concepts, stories, and settings of their world as they understood it. Stories about God would include stories about war and exile because people spent a lot of time experiencing war and exile. Stories about God would be set in a TSU, because that was how the universe appeared to people in that day and age.

As we begin to understand this view of scripture, we realize that it doesn't matter so much whether God exists in a TSU, or in a very large space/time block universe. What does matter is that God exists and that God is the Creator of the universe, no matter how it appears or what model we humans have of that universe. It is quite possible that 2000 years from now, humanity will have quite a different view and understanding of reality than we do. But, even so, the basic story of God's relationship to reality will not have changed because it is this relationship, and the role of God in the relationship, that is the truth of Scripture, not necessarily the precise "science" of the universe as portrayed by Genesis 1.

Put another way, Scripture is what comes into being as the mind of humanity experiences the mind of God and attempts to put that experience into words that people can understand. Our faith asserts that the mind of God is far greater than our minds and that even to touch the mind of God is to risk death from overexposure to the power of God. The experience of God's presence is overwhelming and truly beyond words. Of course this is a problem if God wishes to communicate with us. The solution is to try and explain and describe God using many different types and styles of writing, all of which point beyond themselves to what Paul describes as the mind of Christ.

This vision of Scripture as it relates to both God and reality doesn't mean that the Bible has nothing to say about material reality and what 'really' happened thousands of years ago. One area where this question becomes particularly challenging is in regards to the so called miracles stories in the Bible, particularly the ones that are so central to our faith, such as the resurrection. Some people in the modern era wish to simply dismiss these outright on the grounds that since the Bible isn't a science book, we shouldn't have to worry about whether these miracles 'really' happened. However, this approach is not in keeping with the view that the Bible is a sacred text because the acts of God that we call miracles are saying something about who God is and how God acts in the world.

What we must avoid is a purely mechanical view of these stories. For example the idea that if I pray for some miraculous thing it will happen, because that isn't what the stories in the Bible are about. Rather they point to the reality that God is involved in an ongoing transformation of the world, one that can happen in very remarkable ways. This is consistent with what we know about the universe, namely that surprising things can occur and new properties can emerge seemingly out of nowhere, in a manner that certainly appears miraculous to us.

These reflections give us a good vision of how Scripture can be used and viewed within a non-TSU model of reality. In days when Scripture was written, it referenced the TSU because that was the current literal understanding of reality. This view was used as a framework within which to understand God, the world, humanity, and the relationships between these entities. However, the framework itself wasn't the main point but simply the canvas upon which the action took place. Therefore, as knowledge evolves, we continue to use Scripture as the authoritative revelation of the spiritual nature of reality. Meanwhile our scientific understandings allow us to alter and adjust the framework so that God shines every more brightly through the pages of the Bible.

The contemplative practice of Lectio Divina, or Sacred Reading, is a method of praying with scripture that embraces the Bible as sacred text. This practice once again shows us how the contemplative approach to faith exists in harmony with a non-TSU Christianity.

Rather than seeking 'correct answers' from the Bible, contemplating scripture asks us to listen for the living God who emerges through the text. The truth that is revealed to us in our prayer isn't the truth of ancient video, rather it is the truth of relationship with God. Encouraging communities of faithful to a deeper experience of the divine through this use of the Bible is far more profitable then arguing over where Noah's Ark might be buried.

The last two chapters of the book draw us out into the world as we address the issues of Eschatology and Contemplative Action.

Chapter 11

Eschatology - Mind Freed

When human beings display the tendency to think that we know all that exists, we reveal our ego's ability to prevent us from seeing beyond ourselves. We act as if we truly are the center of the universe and believe we have arrived at the pinnacle of knowledge and technology. This behavior occurs even if we won't admit it in public! Often this pitfall is most clearly seen in hindsight as technology progresses, or when people encounter new technologies across cultures, or if we look back at the history of arguments related to issues in the Church.

In the early 20th century, space travel and undersea submarines were the stuff of science fiction. Hardly anyone thought these things were possible, until they both were accomplished. In the 1960s many people in America were treated to stories of tribal leaders in Africa eating photographs of themselves because they believed that the photo had stolen their soul. In today's American church no one would seriously argue that God wants certain people to be slaves, yet this was a serious conversation a mere 150 years ago.

We know, deep down, that things change and technology and understanding develop yet we rarely allow this truth to inform our world view. How odd that we tend to label something as 'impossible' until the day it happens! One definition of a miracle is something that occurs by means of a technology several developmental steps beyond the current culture's technological know how. The eating of the photograph is a good example of this definition.

This human habit of 'freezing' the state of knowledge in our world is an important background for any discussion of Eschatology. Because the topic of Christian Eschatology deals with the future, our basic instinct is to define and view the future in terms of the present; what we know now and what we understand now. If we think about this approach for only a few minutes we can see it's ridiculous, but it's what we do.

For example, within modern cosmology people speculate about the future course of the universe and many claim that, due to the laws of Thermodynamics, the universe will eventually end by cooling off completely and 'dying.' Some who adhere to this theory say nothing about the possibility of further emerging properties of the universe or of any other unknown change agents or transformations that might occur to alter the future they imagine. They base their models on what we know now consciously, or unconsciously, assuming that this is all there is to know! I once watched a lecture of a physicist proudly describing, with complete accuracy and confidence, and without any hesitation, the next several billion years of our solar systems' development.

Since modern cosmology is only about 125 years old, assuming we know enough to describe the far future is a bizarre assumption. One would think that someone in such a new field would be especially suspicious of making predictions based upon the current state of our understanding. But such is the nature of the human ego. Our limited minds are capable of endless deception.

Christian Eschatology consists of theological statements and claims about what is popularly called, the 'end of the world.' There are numerous models of how the eschaton occurs and what happens as a part of this process, but what all of these visions hold in common is the understanding that God, through Jesus Christ (hence the term 'second coming' that is usually associated with eschatology), will, at some point in the future, enact a final transformation of reality such that the work of salvation begun through the incarnation, death, and resurrection of Jesus comes to fruition, and sin and death are finally defeated once and for all. Furthermore, eschatology usually has some judgement component where by, in an act of final judgement, God sets right all of the wrongs that are yet to be adjudicated.

In these visions and models of eschatology, the TSU takes center stage. In the second coming of Christ, Jesus is seen as coming out of the clouds and the heavens are 'split open' as the dome of the sky is broken apart to make room for God's appearance. Depending on the particular eschatological model in play, people are perhaps taken up into Heaven, or thrown down into Hell as the final judgement is rendered. Earth is also the scene for tribulation, battle, and massive upheaval. Another vision that is also given is that the new heaven and new earth descend from the sky like a giant movie set or something out of an alien movie. This vision posits a city, the new Jerusalem, currently being assembled 'up there.'

Eschatological visions also include statements about what will happen to the dead. Thus the 'general resurrection' envisions a bodily rising of all those who have died as they inhabit this new kingdom. Even though there are several solid scriptural statements which indicate that our resurrection bodies are not like our current physical bodies, people have adopted numerous burial practices and ideas that indicate they still hold a material, spatial view of this transformation. Cemeteries orient graves so that the corpses will 'face east' when the eschaton comes. Many Christians still are afraid of cremation because they wonder how their body will be reassembled during the resurrection. Other questions abound including things like what age will we be when we return, and how will God reattach limbs or remove cancer.

These practices, questions, and concerns, which reflect genuine deep seated feelings and fears about the nature and love of God, arise directly from the TSU model of reality; a model that leans heavily on material spatial images. From a scientific view of the universe most of these images and issues are out dated and even somewhat absurd. However it's important that we not blame people for holding thoughts that were given to them by the Church, which after all claims to propagate and represent the teachings of God. People's questions are a reflection of their faith and their concern for themselves and their loved ones. If the church has done a poor job of educating people then we who work within the church must take responsibility for setting things right.

A non-TSU vision of eschatology must begin by trying to tease out the heart of the matter, the central issue, of this theological topic. The hope of eschatological fulfillment contains at its core a vision of our mind being completely freed. This image of freedom, which of course runs through the entire Biblical witness from Exodus to Revelation, is a freedom in the most fundamental and complete sense. Imagine, if we can, being freed from worry, from fear, from hatred, from every sin or even tendency to sin; imagine being freed from the constraints of illness and old age and ignorance, being freed to love completely and fully. What if we were freed even from the constraints of time and space.

This type of complete freedom is what we normally attribute to God, and any sense that we might gain such freedom would normally be considered impossible. Yet I would suggest that this is exactly what eschatology promises;

we hope that we will be able to be transformed such that we move into the radical freedom offered by God in Jesus Christ.

Such a freedom has certain attributes. The first, and most important in terms of developing a non-TSU model of reality, is that the freedom imagined by eschatology cannot be manifested within a material spatial reality. If we are material we must age. If we are a separate material being we must know the fear of death. If we are a material being we must be constrained by gravity, by space, by time. This means any understanding of the eschaton which relies on, or requires, the resuscitation of our material bodies must be wrong.

Following from this observation, we can say that any model of eschatology that is grounded in *any* material, spatial, image must also be incorrect. If a new city descends from heaven, then are we free to go out of the city? If eschatology consists in us going 'up there' then what if we want to be free to go elsewhere? Any material spatial place by definition sets limits upon us that are inconsistent with the radical freedom of God.

At the same time, an eschatological future that allows us such limitless possibility must somehow also allow us to inhabit space and time in some manner. An end that simply zaps us into nothingness isn't appealing or consistent with eternal existence. As such, we must be both embodied and not embodied to be fully free.

If we put together all of these considerations, what we arrive at is an eschatological vision that understands the eschaton to be the state of a mind that is fully freed and transformed such that the image of God is not only revealed but fully formed and stabilized. In many ways this is similar to what I said earlier about Heaven, but now the entire creation participates in this change.

In such a reality, mind and matter are freed to interact, form, and reform one another such that mind is no longer constrained within time and space yet it can also participate in time and space. This view while potentially consistent with what we currently understand about the nature of the universe, also presents a vision that seems impossible because we do not have, nor do we understand, the mechanism, the spiritual technology so to speak, that would allow such a process. Therefore, those who wish to deny God or the vision of the eschaton, would make the claim that such a view, such a state of being, is impossible.

However, if we look back at the past, we know that the path of history is littered with the claims of impossibility that have been discarded as one vision of truth and possibility after another is fulfilled. While this particular understanding of eschatology is speculative in the sense that the mechanism is not at hand, it is at least consistent with what we now know. Furthermore it is freed from the TSU model which is inconsistent with current knowledge, and poses so many difficulties for believers that they shy away from the promise of radical freedom given to us by a mind fully freed in Christ.

Chapter 12

Bringing it all together:
Ethics, contemplation, and action

The Introduction described the importance of our underlying, often invisible, assumptions about the world around us. This last chapter returns to this issue asking: what difference does a new vision of material reality make in our lives? In addressing this question I want to bring the new vision full circle and ground it firmly in the present moment. For indeed that is all we have. This chapter will explore the implications for our life as Christians in light of the new vision of the universe as it relates to the gospel of Jesus Christ.

The Three-Story Universe model is problematic because it deadens our faith by trivializing Christianity; turning it into a question about which way the elevator goes after we die. Developing a theological model consistent with the current scientific view of the universe brings our faith to life in the present. It helps us see that the point of the gospel is, as Jesus says, to do what He commands; to liberate and realign our mental habits and behavioral patterns here and now, in the communities of the world, such that they are in-Spirited with the mind of a loving God. This new vision also helps us understand how God can be alive, present, and active within our world, not just far off and distant in space, or non-existent all together, the victim of discoveries about the 'laws of nature.'

Yet for many, the connection between our concept of reality and our day to day life is unclear and obscure. Who cares how big the universe is or what my sub-atomic particles are doing? Can such things get me a job or help my sick child or cure the ills of the world? It seems a great leap from one subject to the other. I want to claim, in the strongest possible way, that not only is our understanding of reality important, it is pivotal in determining how we shape the world. Consider these examples:

In my seminary internship I worked with men who were in treatment for domestic violence. Many of them had come from religious backgrounds where God was described as a violent big man up in the sky. When people didn't do what that man wanted, he punished them violently. This image of God, and God's relationship with humanity, helped them justify the violence they were doing when their wives or girlfriends did 'something wrong.'

Currently there is a large group of people who claim to be Christians who are praying for a nuclear world war three because they feel this conflict will bring about the second coming of Jesus. This idea is based upon a TSU understanding of reality in which Jesus is up in the clouds waiting to descend upon the earth in wrath. In this model, the earth is merely a staging area on our way to heaven and a battleground for the spiritual beings who will descend upon us at the appropriate time.

I've mentioned the phrase "pie in the sky when you die," a term denoting the idea that we gain the positive results of faith following our death. This view of reality has been used to excuse all manner of evils from slavery to genocide to greed and corruption. As long as you say you believe in Jesus, you are going to Heaven and the many forms of social injustice here on earth are irrelevant and not worth trying to change.

As these examples show, the TSU model of faith influences, for the worse, the choices we make about how we spend our days, our time, our money. The TSU vision of reality actually encourages the notion that God is far away and not particularly relevant in daily lives. This results in what has been described as functional atheism. The lack of a theological vision of reality that is consistent with what we know of the world results in people living as if they are atheists, even if they say they believe in God.

The hallmark of secularism is that people assume they are fundamentally in charge of their life. When we believe that 'it is all up to us', or when we live as if this is true even if we say we don't believe it, then we have become a functional atheist. If one attends the average church committee meeting or board meeting, what you will see is a group of people trying very hard to 'do the work of the church.' Ask this group what God thinks of their work, and you will often be greeted with blank stares. They have no idea because they haven't done anything to engage God in their process. With such an approach to the life of faith, why are we surprised that churches are increasingly empty? Church is simply one secular option in a sea of secular options, and most of the alternatives are more fun, entertaining, and even enriching.

The TSU, consciously or unconsciously, tells people that God is far away and only marginally concerned with the workings of this world. These conclusions are made more pressing by the science that makes us suspicious of the TSU. Now God seems further away than ever and deep down we suspect that 'He' might not even exist at all. If this is true, then we need to work harder and harder to 'get things done' because if we don't do it, who will? So we plod ahead with our plans and our ideas and our projects and agendas feeling, deep down, that our work is the sole content of a 'real' world.

Thinking that we are alone on this planet not only causes many of the problems of our world, the harmful conflict, alienation, and despair, but also causes much trivial waste of time. If I believe in Jesus and I'm going to Heaven, then why not waste my life watching TV, or endlessly consuming the world's resources, or spend my time doing nothing but increasing my own material good. The TSU vision results in a life on earth that is vacuous, painful, and often lived in fear and isolation. As an alternative, a theological vision grounded in scientific reality offers us a vision of faith that is not only present and life-giving, but is actually more consistent with what Jesus taught.

Looking at the theological model as I've developed it so far, we can see that rather than being driven by spatial descriptions, as is the TSU, the new view is primarily focused upon mental process interacting with material reality. We have come to realize that the time/space home we call our universe comes into being as mind interacts with matter and energy (which are fundamentally one and the same thing) to create stable forms and ongoing reality. Within this universe God's non-material mind acts and interacts with material creation to in-Spirit the world and embody mind within humanity. Although this is an amazing creative endeavor, it also results in the disjunction of our individual minds with the whole of creation, an alienation that God wants healed.

Within this new theological vision, time and space aren't the rigid boundaries that one finds in the TSU. The lines between earth, heaven, hell, salvation, and judgement are no longer dividing lines based upon spatial material existence, but rather are divisions based upon our state of being.

Such a distinction has enormous implications for our day to day life. If our faith and our relationship with God is no longer a matter of later on, of what will happen in the future based upon some intellectual answer to a yes or no question - do you accept Jesus as your personal Lord and Savior? - then the full force of our relationship with God rushes into the reality of the present. Suddenly our state of mind, our relationship to ourselves, our God, our neighbor, becomes the forefront of our faith lives.

Perhaps the objection would be made that this has always been the case, even with the TSU, due to the central role of confession and repentance of sin in our faith tradition. I would suggest that our understanding of these acts of contrition is different when performed against the background of the TSU, versus experiencing them in light of our current knowledge of material reality. In the past, confession and repentance were still highly functional and mechanical and future oriented. You were behaving now so that later a distant God would promote you to Heaven. In addition to the problem that this image disconnected our faith from the present, this functionality and afterlife orientation has also been the source of abusive religion that, among other things, has scared children into believing that if they accidentally died before they confessed a sin they would go to Hell.

The new view, which soon I'll also claim isn't that new, still emphasizes repentance but the orientation of such an act is very different. The transformation of our minds in the present is what pulls us out of Hell and towards Heaven starting right now.

A liberated mind is one that cares only for good. It is one that sees beyond the veil of tears to a mind that patterns nature for life, and thus it is a mind that desires only life and not death. As our faith, in practical reality, transforms our minds, we desire to work for good and be the peace of the world. Through such a change in being we know that the kingdom of God has come near to us and it is in this way that our faith becomes a living faith as opposed to a dead exercise that we participate in once a week, or once a year.

The book of Ecclesiastes claims that there is nothing new under the sun and there is a great truth to this statement. If God is truth, and if science is also the search for truth using the tools of a mind that God gave us, then our 'new' vision of reality is one that should also be an 'old' vision of reality and this is indeed the case. The contemplative tradition of our faith is based upon the transformation of the mind of the believer such that they enter into union with God.

This approach to Christianity developed over the centuries when Christ didn't descend from on high and return to earth as many thought he would. The founders of this movement recognized that the silence of prayer gives our mind an opportunity to encounter the living God. Although these men and women had none of the scientific data or theory to describe why this was possible, or how it was happening, they had the experiential evidence to know that it was true. This is because, as I mentioned earlier, contemplation is in fact very 'scientific'. As these prayers repeated the experiment of aligning their minds with God certain very predictable, repeatable, and amazing things happened. Not only did 'miracles' occur with regular frequency, but, more importantly, communities of people who worked and lived and tried to love together arose and slowly began to transform the world around them. Of course they were always being dragged back into the darkness of a Fallen world, but that didn't dim the importance of their discovery about the value of an examined life.

With our current scientific view of faith, the value and importance of contemplative practice becomes more evident. It's not a coincidence that as our scientific understanding of the world has grown, so has our population's interest in contemplative practice. I've heard many times how people have left the church and gone to a non-Christian retreat center simply because the church couldn't help them develop their contemplative spiritual life. Perhaps people have intuited what I have formally put forth here; we come from the mind of God and it is to the mind of God that we are called.

Understanding that our mind, and our relationship with our mind, is the central focus of our faith life helps clarify one of the oldest sources of theological confusion in Christianity: are we saved by faith or works? This discussion, still common today, and in the world of the church is sometimes heard as a conflict between contemplation and action, also arises out of the TSU model of faith. If our salvation is a decision that will be made at a moment in time by a God up in Heaven, and it's a decision about us going to a place, then what determines that decision: is it what we do, or is it what God gives us?

This question is a source of conversation and confusion because both answers have merit. On the one hand, we want to affirm God's power and grace in salvation, but on the other, we know that salvation must have *something* to do with us. Furthermore, if we affirm too strongly that salvation has nothing to do with our actions, then we truly open the door to a notion that our current time on earth is irrelevant.

This dilemma also exists because of what we read in Scripture. There are many times in the New Testament when both Jesus and some of the writers talk specifically about a link, even a causal link, between faith and works. From James' comment that faith without works is dead, to Jesus' insistence that those who enter the Kingdom are those who hear his words and do them, to Paul's imagery of a foot race, it appears that the Biblical writers understood more clearly than we do that belief and action are closely intertwined.

If we apply the new vision of reality model to this question, much of the conflict and confusion disappears. In a world where mind and matter are uniquely and continually intertwined at every level of reality, faith, a mental process, and works, a material process, cannot be seen as separate acts or endeavors. Our faith and our works and God's work with us move together as one in the nexus between time, space, and mind. To say that one is somehow separate from another is a false distinction that cannot hold up. When I do something good, wasn't it out of the goodness and faith in my mind, and isn't it possible that God put that thought or feeling there to begin with? Furthermore, don't we commonly observe that people who spend much time in prayer are also good and loving people who do wonderful things in the world, and also insist that any good they do comes from God? True faith and true works are from the same source and return to their source, the God who even Jesus claimed was the only One who is good.

Another major issue for our modern era is how people of different faiths should relate to each other in our modern world. This is a large and significant subject that requires its own book. However I do want to briefly address this question here, and point towards some possible avenues of exploration suggested by the new vision of reality.

The standard historical Christian approach to inter-religious relationships arises from the TSU model. In this view, 'our' God - the Christian God - is the only real God and He functions much like a tribal warlord. Thus people of other faiths are worshipping either nothing, because only our God exists in Heaven, or they are worshipping Satan who is the lord of Hell. Within this model, the only good way to approach people of other faiths is to convert them or, if this fails, kill them. This is how Christians have approached non-Christians throughout history and there are many voices in the present day that approach the followers of other religions in this fashion.

Although this view obviously contradicts, on the face of it, much of what Jesus said about love and how to relate to one's enemy, people have found numerous ways to ignore Jesus. Most of these theological arguments appeal to the violence attributed to God in the Old Testament as well as a few New Testament stories and the Revelation of John; but at their core, any such behavior towards others can be traced to our separate ego existence that sees anything and anyone outside of our tribe as a threat and something to change or extinguish.

Any modern view of inter-religious relationship must see beyond this tribal, TSU view and attempt to approach people of different faiths both from the perspective advocated by Jesus, and with an approach consistent with our new understanding of the universe. As I said, this topic is vast so here I will just offer a few starting points for an exploration of this subject.

There is a difference between the specific content of a religion and its ultimate claims or direction and these differences are often confused. We can see such confusion when the 'real' differences between faiths are described in terms of doctrine, or focus, or worship, or some aspect of theology. While such differences are real, they are not necessarily differences in ultimate concern or claim. The theological model of material reality presented here is one that focuses on theological topics with an eye towards issues of ultimate concern rather than the particulars of religious practice. When having inter-religous dialogue it would be helpful to be clear about which level of discourse is being addressed. A difference in religious practice may obscure a similar core assessment of the nature of the universe and our place in it.

The scientific view of reality shows the universe to be unified at every level. We are all interconnected and even every particle across vast space and time are entangled at the quantum level. A modern faith with any integrity must, as it relates to ultimate concerns, incorporate this fact of interconnection, a truth which points in the direction of relationship and reconciliation between peoples. Jesus' command to love even your enemy was his way, in an ancient world, of moving beyond tribalism and relaying the truth that God calls us to participate in a unified reality. If our experience of Hell here on earth is indeed a reflection of God's judgement upon us, then endless killing in the name of religion is not pleasing God one bit.

If contemplation is a practice that occupies a prominent position as we engage a new vision of the universe, then it would be useful to see if contemplation is common in other faiths, and whether the contemplative experience across faiths shares anything in common. Indeed, we find that every religion and every culture throughout history has engaged in contemplative practice. When we examine the teachings and writings of these contemplatives, we find similar conclusions and descriptions about the experience of close human interaction with the spiritual realm. This is consistent with the fact of universal interconnection and we might conclude that all contemplatives, irrespective of the content of their religion, are cultivating union, intense intimate relationship with the mind of God.

None of these observations are meant as the final answer, and none of them negate the truth of our faith.

Regardless of what we may think of other religions, God has only one requirement of us as Christians, and that is to truly *be* Christians, that is enough. Can we actually do what Jesus told us to do? If we can, then we not only begin to enter into the Kingdom of God, but we also provide a true and real example of a new way of being human, a way that is attractive and loving. Although tribalism always sees threats coming from outside the tribe, the biggest threat to our faith is ourselves. When Christians fail to be real followers of Jesus, no one else is interested in what we have to say, and for good reason.

Thus, as I come to the end of this new model of reality I hope two things are clear. The first is that science, and any scientific view of material reality is in no way a threat, or fundamentally at odds with, our Christian faith. The second is that this new view, which in some ways is just an old view, allows our faith to be much more immediate and vital. It also brings into stark focus the responsibility bestowed upon us by this thing we call Christianity. God has given us a mind and God wants us to use it for good and for love and not for evil and for hatred. The choice is ours, as are the consequences of our actions. Grace and judgement are woven into the world in which we live, and God is ever present to inspire us to follow Jesus. For He was the one who fully aligned himself with the transforming and creative power of the universe, and in the process he found eternity and gave it to us as the next step of our voyage.

17013966R00070

Made in the USA
Middletown, DE
26 November 2018